I No Hero

I No Hero

Victor M. Villarreal

iUniverse, Inc.
New York   Bloomington

I No Hero

iUniverse books may be ordered through booksellers or by contacting:

iUniverse
1663 Liberty Drive
Bloomington, IN 47403
www.iuniverse.com
1-800-Authors (1-800-288-4677)

ISBN: 978-1-4502-3421-4 (pbk)
ISBN: 978-1-4502-3340-8 (cloth)
ISBN: 978-1-4502-3339-2 (ebk)

Printed in the United States of America

Library of Congress Control Number: 2010907577

iUniverse rev. date: 6/22/2010

Dedication

I dedicate this book to my father Gregorio Villarreal-Treviño, whose efforts to support and raise us as good citizens paid off for all of us. Even though he was poorly educated he made smart moves and decisions that affected us during our lives. His vision of having a good family paid in good dividends and you can rest assured Dad that we will never let you down.

Acknowledgements

I would like to thank my wife of forty years and mother of our three children Elma Linda Villarreal for her never ending support of this project which was so important to me. There were other persons who supported me in the last two years it took me to write my autobiography entitled I NO HERO.

Others I would like to thank are as follows.

Dr. Rex Ball, Laredo State University (Now TAMIU).

Dr. Stanley Green, Laredo State University (Now TAMIU).

Dr. Rafael Lecuona, Laredo State University (Now TAMIU).

Dr. Dean Champion, Texas AM International University.

Attorney David Almaraz, Laredo, Texas for your advice.

Attorney Dan Ramirez, Laredo, Texas for your help with the computer.

And to my soldiers who kept me alive during the war and who refreshed my memory now some forty years after the war.

Sgt. David Heiner, Delta Pennsylvania, for the pictures and memory of events.

Sgt. Dan Griffin, New York, for the pictures and memory of events.

Spec 4 John Bailey, Encino California for all the pictures you provided and your outstanding memory of events.

Spec 4 Jeffery Spencer, Avon Lake, Ohio, for your memory of events.

Sgt. William(Bill) Mazejko, for the pictures and memory of events.

Lt. Rick Kopec, for your pictures and memory of events.

Lt. Joel Snyder, for your artillery support and pictures and comments.

Lt. Charlie Bader for your pictures and memory of events RIP my friend.

And a special thanks to Dr. Rosa Vida for your encouragement.

Contents

Introduction

It was hard for me to think that when Father decided to immigrate the family to the United States that my life would change so much. Even though the changes were drastic from my point of view they were definitely for the better. I would get the opportunity to go to school and learn English but with that came a new way of life and responsibility . I would grow up in a free environment and enjoy all the benefits of this great country called the United States.

Along with enjoying these new benefits came a big price for me. I would be involved in protecting an help in keeping this country free and strong. I would make hard sacrifices and lose some friends in that thing called the Viet-Nam War but it was all for the good cause. I love this country and I don't regret the hardships made.

CHAPTER 1

Living in Mexico

It was the summer of 1947 in a small ranching community when I arrived on the scene via mid-wife. The community is named "*El Ebano*" after a large shady tree that abounds in the area. The nearest large city is Sabinas Hidalgo, Nuevo Leon, Mexico. It was the 5th of July and in the United States people were just finishing the Independence Day Celebrations (and why not the big war had ended just a few years earlier.)

I was born to Gregorio and Juanita Villarreal and I was their sixth child. The oldest was Gregorio Jr. who was followed by Ofelia and then Roberto who was followed by Cesarita. When sister Armandina was born it was not long after that Cesarita died at the age of two of childhood diseases. Then I was born and shortly thereafter Armandina died also of childhood diseases. Four years after that the last child was born, she was named Lilia. The family never numbered more than seven including my parents.

Father was away working in the United States that summer and it was up to Mom to take care of the kids, run a small store and take care of the milk cows. The cows would be milked daily and they were turned loose to graze in some community acres that were to be used by the village people. The cows would wander down this strip looking for foliage and then return to the home corral daily. Of course their calves were penned up and they would summon the cows with their clamor for milk. Before the calves were fed the cows were milked and the milk was picked up by a milkman who would take the milk to Sabinas to be processed into cheese.

Mom had the choice to name me and she considered many names until one day a relative came to visit who was named Victor. The old boy had been a high ranking officer in the Mexican Army but apparently was a rebel in some way and had been cast away and was now retired. He spent most of his time visiting relatives and telling stories about his military life. Well, thanks to his timely visit, I picked up his name.

Father would occasionally write and send money which was needed to carry on the everyday life on the rural village. He was working in the Rio Grande Valley of Texas for a railroad company that would legally contract workers because of the shortage due to the war. From the Rio Grande Valley he was contracted to a cattle ranch named *"La Tortuga"* (turtle) near Big Wells, Texas. When father was not working in the U.S., he would be home working with the milk cows. He would do a lot of hunting in the nearby ranches and mountains. Deer and turkeys were always on the menu at home. Sometimes Dad and his brothers would go trapping in the mountains for ringtail, a small exotic animal that was harvested for its fur.

Growing up at *"El Ebano"* was a true adventure for me because there were many things to do. When I started crawling, my favorite past time was to wander off from the big *"Jacal"* (which was a large old fashioned home with a thatched roof). We lived in the *"Jacal"* and I would head for the corral pens. Once in the cow pens, I would look for the biggest and freshest cow pie, and well, by that time, I was hungry. By the time my babysitter, who was my older sister Ofelia, would find me, I had indulged in the cow pie. Somehow none of the cows stepped on me. Then as I became more mobile, I wandered down to the *Arroyo El Ebano* which occasionally has running water and boy did it feel good. The village boys were always down there playing and even taking care of the little ones. And then there was looking for frogs, snails and horny toads. Boy! That was a lot of fun.

"El Jacal" where I was born and where Mom had her little store.

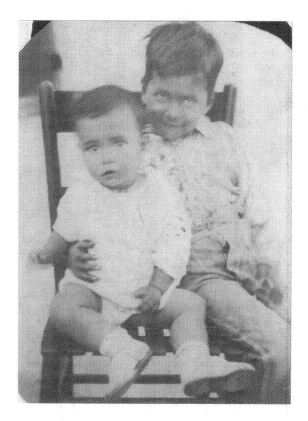

Mom wanted a picture of little Lilia so I had to hold her.

Mom would do her best o always provide at least one gift for each child during the Christmas holidays. She would make us write a letter to Santa Claus and to ask for what we wanted. Everyone was conservative in their requests, except Roberto. His list was always the longest. One year shortly after the big war, he asked for a toy tractor so he could do some planting and not have to use oxen. But the request he made that was very humorous was for a large sack of flour so mother could make us flour tortillas. He explained he was tired of eating corn tortillas, because Mexico was exporting all the flour to the U.S. so they could make biscuits for the *"Gringo* soldiers" fighting oversees. Since eating was a big adventure for me, I was more concerned for a small jar of mayo, but just for me.

picture of the family. Gregorio, Ofelia, Myself and Roberto.

At age five we move to Sabinas and father purchased this large property on the outskirts of the city. We lived next to the *Rio* Sabinas and again I had a built in play ground with the river behind our house. Most of the time the river flowed clear blue water, but even during hard times when it would get stagnant there were many fishing holes that provided fishing and splashing in the water. Moving to the city meant going to school and I was not willing to do that voluntarily.

Sabinas Hidago is located with mountains to the south and west making it very warm in the summer and with semiarid lowlands to the north making it cold in the winter. Having no protection from the north make it windy and cold in some months, but very warm in others since the cool westerly winds do not flow in the summer because of the mountains. The town is blessed with a natural sweet water spring (*El Ojo de Agua*) that flows thru the edge of town and helps with the growing of soft skin avocados. The young women of the area are usually gainfully employed in the numerous dress factories and embroidering bed sheets and pillow cases. The young men who are not employed in the few jobs available there, make their way north to the United States in search of work.

I started first grade at the age of five and hated every moment. School was divided into two buildings. One for boys and one for girls and they were about one block apart from each other. Basically, we never saw the girls unless it was before or after school. The boys' building was like an inclusive fortress. We did basically everything inside until released. I later studied buildings such as these but I think they were called prisons. I hated to go to the bathroom which was a large room with two stools and a long urinal where you stood and peed. The standing there was not bad unless one of the school bullies was there and "accidentally" pushed you into the canal that was usually full of urine. It was no use to complain because it would only get worse.

This picture is of my first grade class in Sabinas Hidalgo.
Note the disparity in the dress, some in winter jackets and some in
short sleeves. I am the first on the left on the third row. My friend
Benito Juarez is the second from the left on the second row.

School would start early and my newly acquired friend Benito Juarez, and I would walk together about two miles to the *"Colegio"* as it was called. At about noon they would release us to walk home (most of the time we were so hungry, that we ran) to return at 3 P.M. and then be released again about 6 P.M. This meant a long lunch break which was done because of the intense heat during the noon hours. This meant eating lunch, doing homework that had not been done, or a quick trip to the river before returning to school. Sometimes getting home meant that lunch was not ready and something had to be purchased from the city. Sometimes a trip to the *"molino"* was necessary. The *"molino"* was a mill where I would take boiled corn kernels and they would mash it for the corn tortillas. The mill was about a block short of reaching the school. My underarms were pretty sweaty by the time we returned to school.

The classroom activities were pretty stringent. Most of our learning involved reading, writing, and arithmetic. Most of the time only the teacher had books and he would read to us on different topics mostly the history of Mexico. Then, there were the writing assignments which involved a lot of writing in those big brown writing tablets. The arithmetic was probably the hardest as it involved a lot of writing problems in the tablet and most of all go to the board and write problems that were dictated by the teacher and have the class correcting or humiliating you, mostly the latter.

Then, there was recess which was a social moment and everyone would talk about the movies they had seen. Most of the discussion would involve the latest Gene Autry movie, and there was Red Ryder and even The Lone Ranger. There was little talk about the Mexican movies; it was mostly the Anglo movies, even though; most of us could not understand English. There was a lot of reading the sub-titles. Then we had to go back to the classroom. There were no organized sports until later years.

Finally, school was dismissed and it was the long walk home, now there was no need to run. Benito and I would continue talking about the western movies as we walked over the long metal bridge over *Rio Sabinas*. From the bridge we would look up and down the river to see where the activity was. Once we spotted other boys playing in the water, we would go home and disappear down to the river to join them. If we had a net we would net the deep water holes for fish. As soon as we caught some we would build a fire and throw the fish on the coals. One boy would get the chore of throwing the fish back into the fire. It seemed the fish would protest the barbecue by jumping out of the fire until the heat killed them and they would get cooked. Then it was time to eat them. Some of the boys would remove the scorched scales and the fish guts. But for this kid who had had lunch in the cow corral, this was a small problem.

At dark we would return home to do our homework and get cleaned up since we smelled of fish. Oh; those were the days. Occasionally we would venture farther up or down the river. Then we would venture into a large orange grove own by a rich man named Antonio Gonzalez who lived in a mansion in the front of the orchard. We would play with his grandsons Cesar and Antonio III, but all the time we were spotting which trees had the bigger oranges. Those trees would play an important part for our visit to the orchard later in the evening under the cover of darkness. Sometimes we would hit some apple trees that they had in front of the main house. We never disclosed to our rich friends what we would do at night because we did not want to lose their friendship. It never occurred to us to ask them for oranges, Hell, they were so rich and nice they would have probably given us the fruit.

One day Dad asked us if we wanted to go to live in the U.S. It seemed that his employer Alvin Blaylock in Big Wells, Texas was willing to sponsor us to legally immigrate to reside in the U.S. Everyone said yes, but I was confused because all my friends were in Mexico, but the jars of mayonnaise were in the United States.

Then the preparations started. First, father had to do the leg work at the American Consulate in Monterrey. There were medical exams to take. Also, there were the visa fees to pay, which were $25.00 dollars for each one of us. The currency had just risen from $8.00 pesos for each dollar to $12.50 per dollar. There were transportation arrangements to be made since we had no automobile. This new adventure was a big hassle and expensive too. Now, we were ready to travel to the United States of America (or as I called it the other side).

CHAPTER 2

Coming to America

It was the summer of 1954 when father finished all the requirements for us to go to the U.S. and as we left via commercial bus to Nuevo Laredo to make the official entry at Laredo, Texas, it started to rain in great quantities. The rain did not dampen our spirits but the Rio Grande River reached flood status and without to much warning it swept away the Bridge at Laredo. Yes, what luck, we were in Nuevo Laredo and there was no longer a bridge to enter the United States. The Corps of Engineers quickly started a portable pontoon bridge and father obtained a job working at the site. We went to live with some relatives in Nuevo Laredo while the bridge was made operational.

Finally, the big day came in September 14, 1954 we were going to be allowed to enter the United States. We had to walk with all personal belongings to the edge of the bridge where a taxi would take us across. As we made our way through the crowds of people near the bridge, my brother Roberto crossed a street with all the bags he was carrying and he did not see a taxicab while trying to cross, and the cab almost ran over him. The driver of the cab yelled at him *"Hey pendejo"* but my brother quickly answered *"Tu madre cabron"*. Those were fighting words and the taxi driver quickly exited the cab to confront Roberto when my father, who was at least six feet and probably 240 lbs, came into the picture in defense of his child. The taxi driver quickly retreated and the confrontation was over. We boarded another cab and headed due north across the pontoon bridge that would go up and down like a roller coaster. There was a lot of yelling and screaming as the old car made its way across the pontoon bridge.

We finally arrived on U.S. soil at the Border Station at Laredo. We were herded inside the building and then to the basement to get lice powder on our heads. After our packets were opened and all information verified we were released and legally admitted residents for permanent residence. Dad went to look for a taxi and off we headed north to Big Wells on H-81 until we reached Dilley, Texas and then west on H-85 to Big Wells.

Well, we were home for a while in the tiny town of Big Wells. It did not seemed too different from Sabinas except there were no shoe shines boys along the main street, or any other street. The big difference was that Mother went to Julian Meridith General Store and quickly came back with flour and mayo. She also has some new goodies named Spam, canned winnies, deviled ham, and canned beef. Man, I thought, these "*Gringos*" think of everything. I thought to myself, and I was resisting this, this is like being in heaven.

Dad took us to visit Mr. Blaylock who lived in a fairly big, white house just off H-85 and then we went to live with Aunt Florinda Martinez. Florinda was one of two of Mom's sisters that lived in Big Wells. The other was Tomasita Munoz. Living temporarily with my aunt was great although her home was not very big, it was nice and warm during the coming winter. Florinda's family had grown and left except for Homero her smallest. Homero would take us everywhere in his old Hudson car. We could not use the trunk, however, because he had it filled with cement blocks so that it would be real low in the back and would have better traction when peeling out.

Reality set in real quick when I found out I had to go to school. Big Wells Elementary was in the middle of the small town and I had to walk to school. School was different in the United States. Here everyone had books and they had a gym to play basketball or games when it was cold outside. Even thought there was no school lunch, they did have a break in the morning. For two cents daily they would give you a small milk or chocolate milk. Boy, this was all right, even if I had to go home for lunch.

Picture of my mother in the middle with her sisters Florinda
Martinez on the left and Tomasita Munoz on the right.

Aunt Florinda had a grandson named Guadalupe *"Pin"* Villarreal and he would walk with me to school. He was about one year older and had his own bike, this gave him status. Ruben Ceniceros who was called *"El Raccoon"* because of the dark shadows around his eyes lived across the street and would also walk with us. Ruben was a very nice person and I would spend a lot of time at his house playing. At school I met Eliseo Talamantes and for the years we lived in Big Wells we became very good friends. His cousin Armando Talamantes was also in the class as was Armando Rodriguez who was a real cowboy even at that young age. Armando lived in the east side of town and always had horses and other animals. There was Onesimo Benavides and Jose Martinez and some girls, one was Gloria Rubio and another was Victoria Talamantes who was a younger sister to Armando Talamantes. We were all in the same grade and Mrs. Picket was our teacher. Mrs. Picket was married to our post-master.

After school, life was a dream for a kid like me. I would rush home and eat a quick snack that mom always had ready, most of the time others school kids would go with me because Mom always had extra food, and if she didn't she would quickly grab a pan and make some *"Guisado"*(stew) and the fresh corn or flour tortillas were always plentiful. After the snack we would go down to the railroad crossing and watch the older people work at the Bowman packing shed. There the workers sorted the vegetables grown in that area and packed them in ice. Then they would be loaded on the railroad cars for shipment to the markets. We always picked up some of the ice that spilled over from the railroad cars. We would use the ice to cool drinking water. We also picked up some of the veggies that were discarded at the packing shed and either ate them on the spot or took them home to be used. During watermelon and cantaloupe season, we made out well.

A farmer named George Webb was a big vegetable exporter in the area and Domingo Escobedo was a local labor boss who would hire the crews to harvest the crops. Escobedo was nicked named *"El Ganzo"* or the goose in English. Although Bowman and several other farmers probably owned most of land and did the planting. It was Mr. Webb and Mr. Escobedo who kept most of the migrant population of Big Wells gainfully employed when they were not up north harvesting other crops. These two men were responsible for putting food on many a table in that town either by giving them jobs harvesting the crops or by donating the extra veggies to the workers.

Dad would take us to *"La Tortuga Ranch"* where he worked often and life was great there. We would fish or catch turtles and frogs at the big earth tack near the ranch house. We would go to "La California Farm" nearby and get drinking water in a metal tank sitting on a trailer. While there Dad would buy us a little ice cream cup, my favorite was strawberry. Dad would go hunting and bring either deer or wild hogs for the family to eat. One day while out feeding "Cubes" to the steers, I decided to ride on the truck tailgate on the way back to the ranch house. I was singing and having a ball when Dad hit a bump on the road and I flew out of the truck and landed on the dirt ranch road. When the shock was over I realized that the truck was gone and I had been left behind. I panicked, I could picture the big wild boars coming and eating me. Finally, Dad noticed and came back for me. WOW! What a relief to see my dad.

Life was very simple in Big Wells, Texas in the early 50's. The population was probably close to a 1000 residents of which nearly 800 hundred were migrant workers who would go up north to harvest crops in the spring and return to Big Wells in the fall. Most families would return with money and many were driving new "Chevy" truck or cars. During the fall there were many Jim Walter homes placed on empty lots and sometimes with a new truck or car next to them. However, as the months went by, some of the new trucks and cars were seen being pulled off by "Repo" wreckers. Some of the homes disappeared before they were totally finished victims of the "Repo" companies. This was not unusual as the cycle would repeat itself the following year.

Across from the Bowman Packing Shed, a great pond would form and the water would collect there getting stagnant. Surrounded by the railroad tracks on the south and Main street on the west, the pond would extend for several hundreds yards to the east toward the Benito Talamantes home. It was about one hundred feet in width and several feet deep. This pond soon got stocked by crawfish and they quickly became part of my steady diet. When everyone realized that if I was missing I was at the pond with a string and a wad of dough catching crawfish. I would carry a light frying pan and some lard. I would build a small fire and as I caught them threw their tails into the frying pan.

"Boy", were they good to eat. I made many a friend with my seafood platter. Onesimo Benavides was usually the first to arrive since he lived a mere block away followed by Ruben Ceniceros, Eliseo and Armando Talamantes. If Armando Rodriguez was not riding his horses he also show up, sometimes even with the horse.

Who could ask for more but, life is not always that easy. Just like there had been bullies in the school in Mexico there was a group of boys who did not like me here, and again I was the recipient of some of their hate. While in school they would call me names especially by a derogatory name "*Mojara*" which although it means fish they were using more to describe me as a "Wetback" Their usual chant was "*Mojara*"(fish) or "Wetback" "go back to Mexico where you belong". It was not only annoying but to me it was demoralizing. Soon, the chants developed into a more physical type of harassment as I began to receive an occasional shove or punch. That became a ritual on Fridays as I would receive my weekend special and sometimes a beating was the special of the day.

One Friday afternoon, I was in class with Mrs. Strait, who was a kind little lady and would always treat me well. One of the bullies was doing his usual verbal abuse on me calling me different names, which added up to the same thing, that I was not wanted. "My God", I thought, "When is it going to end"? Are these boys going to harass me for years? Then the bell rang and everyone ran out of the classroom yelling goodbye to Mrs. Strait. I was in no hurry because I knew that at least one bully was going to wait for me outside, after all it was Friday.

Mrs. Strait noticed I stayed behind, so she asked me, what was wrong. I spoke broken English by then and answered that everything was O.K. She responded that if I was worried that the bully was waiting for me outside, and I lied and said no. She summoned me to her desk and in the kindest way, tried to calm my fears. Mrs. Strait went on to tell me that eventually everything would be alright. That what was happening was part of growing up and that it would end soon.

She went on and told me I was a good boy and that one day I would grow up and join the Armed Services. She said that the U.S. would get involved in wars every fifteen years or so. She finished by saying that I would grow up, most likely join one of the services, go to war and return a veteran, may be even a war hero.

When she said that, I pictured myself holding a machine-gun like Robert Taylor in the movie "Bataan". I got very sentimental and in broken English I blurted "I no hero, Mrs. Strait". I ran out of the room fighting back the tears as I had gotten very emotional. As I stepped out of the building I spotted one of the bullies hiding in the laurel shrubs. I knew what was going to happen so I straightened up and wiped my tears. I knew I would be shedding some new tears soon. As I walked toward the school exit and the bully, my friend Armando Rodriguez just appeared out of nowhere and started to chat with the bully. All of a sudden the bully disappeared and Armando headed toward his house and I for mine. I never knew the context of the conversation but the bully days were over for me. I was never harassed at that school again. Thank you Armando, for whatever you told the bully.

CHAPTER 3

The Migrant System

One day, Dad told us that for the summer months we were going to the Rio Grande Valley and pick cotton because the wages he was earning were not enough to sustain the family. We did not have a vehicle so he asked Mr. Armando Rodriguez (father of the younger Armando Rodriguez) to take us to Harlingen where mother had a step-brother named Alfonso Mireles. Alfonso would place us in the same farm where he worked planting cotton. At the farm we were housed in a big house used for the workers which had many double bunk beds. I wanted to sleep on the top bunk and my brother Roberto was on the bottom bunk; however, that only lasted one night because he accused me of wetting the bed and getting him wet.

During the day we worked in the fields all day picking cotton. The humidity was unbearable and we drank a lot of water. I spent most of the day either drinking water or bringing some to my family members so they would not waste time walking to the water deposit. Cotton here was pulled from the plant so that the plant could be picked again. It was hard work but with the whole family working we were able to earn more than dad would earn for Blaylock back in Big Wells.

One Sunday we did not work and when I woke up I looked out the window and saw the strangest thing. There were people on the highway next to the house either walking, some even on crutches, others on their knees all headed south. It was hard for me to understand why these people were doing this, it seemed like they were being punished. Not being able to stand it any more, I went toward the highway and asked them what they were doing. I was shocked to find out that they were doing this voluntarily. They were on a pilgrimage of some promise they had made to the Virgin of San Juan. It seemed that the Church of San Juan was down the road to the south of where we were. I did not know that this activity went on every day, because we were not there the other days when we were in the cotton fields working.

When the work ended at the farm in Harlingen we went with some other families to other cotton farms to the north near Victoria, Texas. Once we ventured over to Bryan, Texas. Little did I know that many years later, I would visit my son, Mark, at Texas A and M University at the same place. One day we went to town and came back with a beautiful black Chevrolet pickup. Boy O Boy, now we had our own vehicle. Dad quickly made a military canvas with some poles into a shelter for the back of the pick-up. Now we could travel to town on our own and we could all go on Sundays shopping for groceries and clothes.

The small cotton towns in Texas were packed with families that were picking cotton and would gather in the small plazas in the towns. There were merchants selling house wares, blankets, clothes and other necessities. There were musicians entertaining and food vendors selling quick foods including some new items to us that were called hamburgers and hot dogs. To me it was funny that hamburgers did not have ham, but they were good and they had mayo and another new item called mustard.

We roamed the small Texas towns sometimes working only a few days before we had to move on. One Sunday as we did our shopping for the week in one of those small towns my brother Roberto disappeared among all the migrants workers. It was time to go since Mom had already purchased some meat items and they had to be put in an ice box with a block of ice to prevent spoilage. Roberto was nowhere to be found so Dad went after him and I did not want to be in his shoes when he was found. After about an hour they both appeared and Roberto was smiling and for the most part so was Dad. Mom broke the party by asking where they both had been, but before Dad could speak Roberto took the lead.

Roberto, who was quick with words, said he was in the plaza watching some musicians play when he noticed a small crowd of people. He approached the group only to find Dad talking to a blind guitar player. It seemed that Dad wanted the man to play a special song about a girl with green eyes that had gone away. The blind guitar player told Dad he did not know it, but if Dad would hum it or sing the words he would put the music to it. According to Roberto Dad started to sing out loud about a girl with green eyes who had gone away and never returned. It was hard for us to picture Dad singing in front of a group since he was a very shy and quiet person. We all laughed but Mom went into a rampage about the story. She gripped all the way back to the cotton farm, and that went on for several years. Apparently, Roberto struck a delicate part of our parent's lives.

Our travels took us to West Texas following the cotton crops. It seemed the more we traveled west that the cotton plants grew smaller and smaller. We visited towns like Plainview, Littlefield, and Levelland and followed the white gold called cotton. It was hot during the day and cool at night. The living conditions were about the same but out west the farmers all planted a garden for the employees. Corn, green beans, cantaloupes and watermelons were everywhere.

One night we were housed away from the garden the farmer had planted for the workers, however another farmer lived across the farm road a few hundred yards away. We could see the huge watermelons and Roberto and I swore we had never seen such melons. A night raid was in order to the melons to see which ones were ripe, so after dark Roberto and I slipped under the barbed wire fence and started to thump the melons. After a while a German Sheppard started to bark and the farmer woke up and turned the light on. I clearly heard him ask his wife for the shotgun. "Those Mexicans are stealing my prize melons" he told his wife. "Leave them alone, it's probably those new kids across the road", she answered. Our hearts were in our throats thinking this man was going to come out blasting. Finally, he turned off the lights and went to sleep.

We crawled back across the road with two of the biggest melons we had ever seen. All of us ate and ate again. Then it was my turn to clean up and get rid of the evidence. I labored until every seed was picked up and then I threw them in the outhouse. Early next morning everyone went to the fields except me since I had stayed up late cleaning the crime scene.

In the morning there was a knock on the door and I answered it, only to find the farmer standing there. "Hey Kid, last night someone stole some of my watermelons and I followed the tracks to your yard", he said. "Yeah, I herd some activity but it was probably aliens eating in our yard last night, but they left during the night", I answered. The farmer looked around the yard and headed toward the outhouse. About half way to the small building he turned around and left. That was pretty close, so we never took someone else's melons again in West Texas.

After the summer months passed, we returned to Big Wells, and Dad went to work for Bowman Cattle Company since Mr. Blalock was somewhat sore at us for leaving to go to the cotton fields. Dad and one of my brothers took turns working near "La Rosita" which was the main Bowman headquarters. The Nueces River flowed nearby and Dad and either Gregorio Jr. or Roberto would burn prickly pear to fatten hundreds of steers that the rancher owned. The cacti that they were burning were huge since the vegetation near the Nueces was also very tall.

There were hundreds of rats living on the cacti and the big rattle snakes would be waiting for the rats to exit the nests to eat them. It was very dangerous being near the cacti camps because of the rattle snakes. My brothers made a game out of who would kill more snakes with the pear burner (flame thrower) during his four day tour. I would ride out to the ranch with the brother that was coming on duty and then ride back to Big Wells with the one getting off. Dad would always stay at the ranch. He either never got tired or he did not want to leave the boys alone.

On Sundays we would go to "La Rosita" to fish off an old abandoned bridge across the Nueces River. After fishing we would finish the day catching armadillos which were plentiful near the river. Dad's brother Bernardino and his family which were Abraham, Maria and Juanita lived at "La Rosita Ranch" and they would join us in the armadillo roundups. Juanita was the thinnest and fastest and would catch more armadillos than the rest of us. The armadillo catching consists of running after them and flipping them over, making them helpless and unable to move. Then, there is the chore of gutting and cooking them into *"Chicharones"* which are a delicious food made from these critters deep fried in their own fat and then strained. And the best part is to get a flour or corn tortilla and make a taco out of the fried meat.

One day Dad came home with another venture, that we would go to Fort Wayne Indiana to work the crops there. We left for Indiana and after driving for a couple of days we arrived. The trip was not without mishaps as we broke down in Little Rock, Arkansas. We parked the truck on the sidewalk somewhere downtown and waited till morning. Dad was worried and could not sleep so he sat on a city bench to think. I was crowded in the back of the truck and I went to sit with him. Also there was the problem with Roberto who would go to sleep and then sub consciously start pinching who ever was within reach. Dad and I talked about just everything including what we were going to do when we got to Indiana.

Sometime during the night the fog set in and it was hard to see for more than a few feet. Dad and I heard voices but we could not see anyone. Finally, the voices got closer and all of a sudden we were surrounded by midgets with lunch boxes. Dad and I looked at each other and thought we were dreaming until a city bus stopped in front of the bench and they all climbed on the bus. We were confused and wondered where the midgets had come from. Well, about thirty minutes later we heard the voices again and the same thing happened, another large group of midgets came out of the fog and climbed on another bus. This went on for several other groups until we learned to ignore them. Finally, the fog lifted and I saw a sign across the street that read "Little People Village", and I realized we were in front of a midget colony and that they were boarding the bus to go to work.

We arrived at Fort Wayne and several of my cousins that lived there came to greet and direct us to the Sweet Farms outside of the city. My fathers' sister Julia and her husband Ruperto Treviño lived on the farm with their family. There was Lupita who was married and had two kids named Elva and Rene. Then there was Jose Angel, Benito, Pedro, Clem, and Ruperto Jr. who was my age. An older daughter Isabel had married and had stayed in Mexico. We were assigned a nice home by Pete Smith the foreman of the farm. The house was so big it had room for another family and when uncle Bernardino showed up with his wife Gregoria and their children Abraham, Maria and Juanita they settled in quite comfortably on the other side of the house. There was a nice garden behind the house and uncle Bernardino and my brother Roberto divided the land and quickly planted a garden.

Picture of brother Roberto and cousin Abraham at the water pump where "Harvey" was killed.

Picture of cousin Maria, sister Ofelia and cousin Juanita and the two station wagons we had.

Picture of Me, Lilia, Mom, Juanita, and Maria
and a fresh crop of pinto beans

Picture of Lilia, Juanita, Ruperto, Maria and
Rene(kneeling), Clem and I with the Sombrero.

Sweet Farms was a thriving enterprise and only fancy veggies were grown there. There were fields of celery, egg plant, cauliflower, radishes, bell peppers, and squash. Dad, Gregorio Jr., Ofelia and Roberto would work in the fields while Mom and Lilia stayed home. My job was to take my family their mid-morning snack and afternoon refreshments. These were long days and the workers would only come home for a quick lunch. I was curious why women wore bonnets made out of cloth to protect them from the sun and I soon found out due to the long days out in the sun.

The workers spent a lot of time on planting machines planting cauliflower and celery. When they saw me coming with their refreshments was the only time they stopped working, so Mom made sure she put some extra tacos for the tractor operator pulling the planters. On some Saturdays and Sundays when everyone was off and going to town Dad and uncle Bernardino would go work for Pete Smith on a farm he had purchased on his own.

In Indiana there were schools so I had to attend them. The bus would pick us up and transport us to the city schools. The bus would come and at the entrance to the farm would pick us up. There were several other families who lived at the farm and the kids would also attend school. Besides the Treviño cousins and the Doroteo Vasquez family there was the Galvan family and of course Pete Smith's kids and I. School was more of a drag here because there were very few people who could speak Spanish. We had to speak English all day long.

One day one little girl got a cultural shock. It seemed that we had to take our own lunch to school and Mom was not used to sending me to school with a lunch bag. The first day the teacher fed me from I don't know where, but I was told to take a lunch the next day. I informed Mom that I needed a lunch bag for me. When I got to the classroom I was instructed to put my bag with the others on a window sill. By lunch time I was starved and at the teachers command we ran to the window and grabbed our lunch bags and headed for the lunch room. There I opened the bag and ate a bologna sandwich, a bag of chips and a very small apple.

Then the fun began, because I had eaten someone else's lunch and there was a little girl crying because the only bag left on the window had what looked liked like a gondola full of greasy food. At that time she did not know that it was a flour tortilla full of egg and sausage. The teacher asked who had eaten the girl's lunch and I did not confess. I told Mom not to ever put tortillas in my lunch because they would discover the sandwich thief.

When Dad was off on Sundays he would take us to Fort Wayne to do shopping and go to the movies. I saw some good movie shows entitled Giant, Partners and State Fair. Sometimes we would go to the City Dump where Dad knew the operator there and he would let us "Shop" through the trash to look for toys and other usable stuff. We only knew the man by "*Chalapa*" and his wife as "*La Gringa*". After the man closed the dump he would invite us to his farm outside Fort Wayne. There he and his wife lived on some acreage and they had a large earthen pond. The farm had a few animals the man had acquired and would always ask Dad how to treat and take care of them. The pond was more of a giant mud hole and there were at least one hundred geese and ducks quaking all over the place.

Mom and "*La Gringa*" would sit on the porch for hours talking. We don't know what they talked about since the lady could not speak Spanish and our Mom could not speak English; yet they managed to converse for hours. By the time it came time to go, Lilia and I had sampled all the food in the house. The lady would also give us food to take with us including duck and goose eggs which smell so bad when you cook them; after all, those birds would be eating mud and rotten veggies the man would bring them. When you cooked one of those eggs everyone around wondered who had pumped one.

There was a family that lived near the farm who had a pet raccoon named "Harvey". Cousin Ruperto Jr. and I would get off the school bus with them and played with the critter. They had a little house for him and he was chained so he could not leave. One winter night Roberto went to get water from the pump outside the house and on a wood pile he had amassed near the pump two eyes jumped at him from the dark. He grabbed a piece of wood and went on the offensive. He came back to the house with the water and his trophy which was a big fat raccoon. Dad quickly skinned the critter and announced there would be "*Chicharones*" for breakfast.

Next morning the "*Chicharones*" were ready and Mom was making fresh flour tortillas as we sat at the big table for breakfast. Man! The freshly made tortillas with the meat inside and with the fresh hot sauce were good. What could be better, but wait there is a knock on the door and Dad tells me to get it. I answered the door because no one said no to Dad. My friends from down the road were there. They said, "Victor, Harvey broke his chain last night and we followed his tracks in the snow to your wood pile, but they disappeared there". There I was with a flour tortilla full of Harvey in my hand and a lump in my throat; I lied to them and told them I had not seen him.

I closed the door and I looked toward the table where no one had missed a bite. I saw Dad, Greg Jr., Ofelia, Roberto, and Lilia devouring Harvey. The only one that was innocent of the crime was Mom because she was busy making tortillas but then she had cooked him. As I approached the table, I placed my tortilla down on the plate and started to walk away. To me it appeared that my family were like a pack of lions sitting around eating one of my friends. Dad was the first to notice the change in me and asked what was wrong and what did the kids at the door want. I blurted out almost in tears "That's Harvey you are eating". The rest of the lions kept on eating, even little Lilia.

Dad, looked at me and in a very serious tone said, "This changes the plan. Victor you will have to bury the hide", and he resumed eating. How can they continue to eat my friend? If they were not my family I could learn to dislike them real fast. And why did I have to do the dirty work of burying the hide. It was Roberto who killed him. Well, I wrapped the hide very well and put some lime on it and then threw it in our out house. I figured when it started to rot, no one would suspect the smell, after all, that was an out house; not a perfume factory. That night, I dreamed that I had been arrested for the murder of Harvey and the police had made me dig up the hide. What a dream!

One evening Gregorio Jr. had gone to town with some older boys at the farm and on the way back the driver fell asleep and crashed against a cement embankment. Gregorio was seriously injured with head trauma and a broken leg. That slowed our trips into town because Mom was afraid that we could have another accident.

At the end of the farm road near our farm was another family who had a small farm and a herd of pigs. The man was named Maco Montalvo and he and his wife had a daughter and three boys. Besides the pigs that we used to amuse ourselves with, they had a television and every Saturday morning we would watch the westerns shows. There was Bob Steel, and Haplong Cassidy and a host of other cowboys. Also on Saturdays Maco would take the boys and Ruperto Jr. and I to a grocery store where they gave him old expired food for the pigs. We would load up and some of the food was consumed by us on the way back.

School in Indiana was O.K. but no one stood out, maybe because there were no bullies at the schools. Everyone seemed content, the teachers were all Anglo and they talked mostly of the political races for President etc. Maybe the absence of bullies was due to the fact that most students came from the farms and every one had something to do after school and we were saving our energies for after school activities. Perhaps bullies thrive when students have too much time on their hands. At least there seems to be a connection that exists there.

We spent two years there in Fort Wayne and Dad purchased a new Ford station wagon. It was candy apple red and white in color inside and out. It was a beauty and now we rode in style. Everyone rode inside and although it did not have air conditioning it was very comfortable and a three seater. Boy, this migrant farm style might not be so bad after all. Now, I could ride inside and be near a window. I could now read all the road signs to practice my English. And of course I read them out loud to annoy everyone since I was the only one who spoke English.

Well, with the new station wagon, Dad felt we should try working in California because the weather was more appropriate for agricultural work. In California he and my older siblings could work all year and they did not have to cope with the snow in winter. To me Indiana was just beginning to feel good, except for the chopping of wood for the winter months. The snow did not bother me much because I learned to do things indoor like playing bingo and whittling. On Saturdays I would go watch the westerns at the Montalvos. Then, there was also the harvesting of mushrooms that we sold to the hunters.

Picture of brother Gregorio at Sweet Farm

Picture of Lilia, Mom, Carlos, and Me with little
Nora by my Mom at Dad's ranch in Mexico.

CHAPTER 4

California Here We Come

California, here we come! We took off from Sabinas where we
had gone to replenish our Mexican supplies like *masa harina,*
chorizo, carne seca, and tequila, yes, tequila. My father never drank, but
sometimes he was so sore and tired from working in the fields that he
needed a sip of tequila in the mornings, sort of a recharge or jumping
cables to start a car.

During this trip back to Texas and Mexico, my sister Ofelia got
married to her boyfriend Carlos Juarez and she stayed in Texas at Big
Wells. She would remain behind and start her new life. Now, it was
Dad and Mom and Gregorio, Roberto, Lilia and I.

And then away we went toward the west. Instead of green vegetation
and lots of trees, we saw desert and a lot of cacti Boy, this is different,
and so I kept on reading the road signs and agitating everyone. Then
we came to the Indian Territories and it seemed that they were selling
all kinds of trinkets. Were these the same Indians I had read about;
the proud warriors who roamed the west and slowed the expansion of
western lands? Now, these proud warriors were making fake arrowheads
and Indian jewelry.

One night on the way to California we were tired and decided to
pull over and rest at a rest area. Roberto had lost his immigration visa
card on that trip and we needed to get him a new one as soon as we had
a mailing address. We quickly spread out on the picnic tables and on the

ground nearby to sleep. Sometime during the night we were visited by the United States Border Patrol. One of the agents woke me up with a nudge of his boot. Mom, woke up and passed the immigration cards to us. Roberto quickly grabbed mine and I was left to fend for myself.

The agent that woke me up wanted to know where my card (*mica*) was. The other agent told him to leave me alone but Mr. Rude insisted on questioning me. Finally, the other agent told him that apparently I was the only one without a card, but I was just a kid and was the only one speaking English. Finally, they left and I retrieved my card from Roberto, who had a big smile on his face, and why not after all he had thrown me to the wolves.

Well, after crossing the state of Texas, New Mexico and Arizona, we crossed into California. Nothing really changed; there was more desert and sagebrush and now an occasional cactus. We crossed most of California and then we started to see greenery and some fruit trees. I could not get over the numerous fruit orchards along the road covered with fruit. Here there were no forests, just groves of the fruit trees and Roberto and I wondered if the farmers knew we were coming. We kept on going through beautiful places like Fresno, San Jose, Bakersfield and then on to Centerville, California.

At Centerville, Dad quickly found work at Granger Farms and Mr. Granger took us to the house we would live in. It was an old barn-like structure, but it was very roomy Mom quickly started to clean the building and we settled in for the stay. It was quite easy to figure out why the town was called Centerville. It was in the middle of a farming area and there were several towns very close by. There was Mission San Jose, Irvington, Decoto, Alvarado and Newark all very close by. Later some of these towns were incorporated into Fremont and Union City, California. There were *Mexicans, Filipinos, Chinese* and *Japanese* everywhere. And then there were *Portuguese, Germans, Polish* and many other nationalities in that area.

Every kind of vegetables and fruits were grown here. There were apple and pear trees everywhere. The most common was the apricot tree, which was new to me, but never less very good to eat. The apricot trees were everywhere also. Right next to our house there were lettuce fields, cabbage, pickle and lima beans fields. We would roast the big lima beans on the stove and eat them as we sat in the evening listening to Dad tell us stories, and for a quiet man he was a good story teller. Mom was cooking away or preparing what she was going to cook for the next day. Occasionally we had single men who would come eat with us and pay Mom a few bucks. Mostly, she did it because she felt sorry for them since their families were back in Mexico.

At the Granger farm there were three houses and another family lived across the road from us. It was Salvador and Celia and their three kids. Celia was a great cook and would always invite me to eat with them, and I always said yes. She would make these huge flour tortillas and several kinds of hot sauces especially one with green *tomatillos*. While she was cooking I took care of the three boys so that was a nice arrangement. They lived in a house that was smaller than ours that was like a windmill from Holland. I liked it because it had two floors and we would go upstairs and see the workers in the fields.

Mr. Granger was a red headed man and very nice to me. He would always stop his truck and talk to me. He was a World War II veteran who had been shot several times in the buttocks. He had a strange walk and it was easy to understand why. Sometimes he would just stare at nothing in particular for a long time. Some of the older workers who had been there longer said that he had been wounded very seriously in the Pacific and that his best friend had been killed. When he was recovering from his wounds he was told his friend had left him the farm when he died.

One day Mr. Granger came and picked me up and took me to the front of the farm which faced the highway toward Centerville. There he was building a fruit and vegetable stand to market some of his products. The rest were trucked to the docks at Oakland for shipping. He unfolded his plan to open the fruit and vegetable stand during the summer months when I did not attend school. He said I was to the in charge and that occasionally he would come by and check on me. I was to sell and restock the veggies for the next day. He explained that since the stand was near the house Mom could bring me lunch and I could eat there.

Everything was planned out by Mr. Granger very carefully. I thought he had left one small detail, and that was how much I was going to get paid. He explained that since I was ten years old he would start me out at ten cents an hour and if everything went well he would raise it to eleven cents the following year. I gave him a hard stare and responded "Mr. Granger, I may be a ten year old kid, but I am not a dummy, I won't work for those wages". He was very surprised at my response and dropped me off to walk home, and the fruit stand never opened. I felt bad every time we drove by and the stand was there, empty, but I never gave in to his wages and I guess he did not want to pay any more than that.

One day I went to the fields to take some lunch to Dad and Roberto who were working cutting lettuce. The lettuce wagon was being pulled by a tractor and the driver was a Puerto Rican man. I asked him if I could drive the tractor and he agreed and stepped down to cut lettuce. At that time Mr. Granger showed up and stared at me on the tractor. After a short while I got brave and asked him how much he was going to pay me. He smiled and started to walk away; then, he turned suddenly and said "Nothing". I guess Mr. Granger had won that round of negotiations.

In Centerville I was going to have to go school and the nearest school was Alviso Elementary School. It was located on the Centerville Highway almost at the expressway from San Jose. Some kids came from the Alvarado area. Most came from a subdivision of new houses near Centerville. The surrounding farms provided a good number of students like me that were either children of the workers or owners of the farms.

Alviso, was a great school because the atmosphere was very relax and conducive to learning. The kids were excellent and the teachers were great. I never had a bad teacher at Alviso and the older gentleman that was the Principal, Mr. Stivers was great. He had a mean look like Broderick Crawford of the old Highway Patrol series, but he was a gentle and great person overall. Mr. Paulsen was our coach and music teacher and was a very good role model. He could kick the football from one end of the field to the other end, or so it seemed to us.

My favorite teacher was Mrs. James followed by Miss Pierce. Mrs. James was pregnant when she was our teacher, but she was very good with us and it helped that she was one beautiful lady. Her husband was in the Coast Guard and would visit us in uniform and tell us stories. Miss Pierce was a very tall, blond teacher. She could arm wrestle all of us, and beat us because she was so big and strong. This school had a cafeteria and several ladies would cook our meals fresh every day. Boy, the food was great and the ladies would always allow me to go back for seconds.

One day we put on a musical play for the parents. The play was Oklahoma and we practiced every day, sometimes after school. I was not a good actor so Hunsi and I were the curtain boys. However we were allowed to peek at the audience at the end, and they even announced our names. Well, I guess that was O.K. Alviso always had neat little programs and everyone behaved well. It seemed that these programs were meant to unite the student body.

Mr. Paulsen would always play beautiful music to us as he would give us writing assignments. We learned to love the concertos he would play for us. One day he assigned us to write about our future careers. Most of the kids wrote of going to a good university and then going into engineering and space programs. For me there was no chance of even going to college so I was at odds what to write about. I decided that I would write about my desire to be a soldier. I wrote my theme and then had to read it to the class.

Some of the kids laughed about my choice, but Mr. Paulsen who knew about my economic condition defended my choice. He went on to explain that being a soldier was good and that many soldiers were needed to keep our way of life secure. He went on to say that I would most likely make a good soldier and that he would be proud of me when that happened. I knew I was just writing to fulfill an assignment.

We did not have organized sports but we did play sports within ourselves. We played football and softball and even some basketball. We ran laps and even long distance within our school grounds. One day Mr. Paulsen started us on throwing passes from one line to the other. It involved getting all the boys in two lines facing each other and throwing the football from one to the other across a distance of about thirty yards. The ball tossing went fine until it was my turn to throw. I threw to the only boy that resembled a bully in the entire school. His name was John and no one really looked forward to playing with him because he had a bad temper.

Well, I threw the ball and it sailed straight to him but he was looking to where the girls were playing and the ball hit him smack in the face. Everyone laughed except him, and within seconds he ran across to my spot and wham! By the time Mr. Paulsen got there I was knocked out. I don't know what he hit me with, but I went down and did not get up. I heard ringing of bells in my head for several months. From then on I called him "Big Bad John" after a song released about that time about a man with an iron fist.

Living in California was great; the weather was really nice and pleasant. Most of the days were breezy and cool. It seldom was muggy, even when it rained. It was nice during the day and cool in the evenings. The weather was very conducive for the growing of crops. It was very rare when Dad and the older boys could not work because of bad weather. And for a young kid like me it was like living in paradise, because I could wander every day after school and during the summers also.

Since we did not own a television, I had a lot of time to read. I would go to the Traveling Library which came to Alviso and check out as many books as I wanted because Mr. Stivers had authorized it for me. He said a kid without television should read a lot, and sometimes I would read as many as seven books every two weeks. I read a lot about hunting and westerns took a lot of my time. The books written by Jules Vern and Mark Twain were great for me. Reading about the *Mysterious Island* written by Vern was fascinating to my young mind. *Tom Sawyer* and *Huckleberry Finn* by Mark Twain kept me thinking that I was somewhat between these two characters. I always figured I was an adventurer like Tom but on the mischievous side like Huck.

Other book characters that captivated my mind were *Kit Carson* and *Jim Bridger*. I was enlightened by the way they roamed the west and trapped and hunted. I figured my Dad had been somewhat like that when he was a hunter and trapper in Mexico. Since I had seen the deserts and mountains when traveling to California I could easily relate with these great men and what they must have gone through in exploring the west and northern regions. R*iders of the Purple Sage,* by Zane Grey was one of my favorites.

At Alviso School I quickly made friends. John Tachala and Tony Silva were my best friends. These were clean cut boys who were interested in their school activities. They were studious and very well mannered. We would play during our recess and before school started. Most of the time we had to ride the bus after school so there was no time for playing.

Occasionally we would meet on the weekends, but most of the time other activities close to home kept us from meeting on weekends.

For a short while we moved from Granger Farms to near Mission San Jose on the other side of Centerville and Irvington. We found a place to live and I attended Olivos de Guadalupe School. I had to walk to school on this road that was lined with olive trees. The olives would go unpicked and we had to basically squash them with our shoes on the way to the school. By the time we reached school our tennis shoes were wet with the milky substance.

When we were at this location Dad worked near Irvington at a farm there. We lived outside of town and there were several families that lived there. My sister Ofelia and her husband Carlos joined us there and we were a complete family again. Carlos' parents and two brothers Jose and Robert joined us and by now sister Ofelia had a baby girl named Nora.

Near our house, lived the Francisco Martinez family who had many chickens and other domestic animals. They had five children, their oldest daughter Connie was married to a man who owned a Chinese market. They had a son named Frank Jr. and three other daughters. The daughters were Maria Elena, Antonieta and Marta. The girls and I would be picked up by a man who would take us to pick strawberries for a cannery. We were paid miserable wages and most of us earned three dollars daily and sometimes had to pay for the ride to work. The enjoyable part was that we talked and sang the latest songs all day long.

One day after school Antonieta and Marta were walking on one side of the highway and some boys and I were walking on the other side but we were still talking to each other when there was no traffic. Suddenly, I saw this big rock on my side of the road and I ran and picked it up. I yelled at the girls "Look, how far I can throw this rock". I threw it way in front of the girls but still in their general direction. About halfway across the highway the big rock hit the highway and changed directions. I looked in horror as the rock changed directions and went and hit Antonieta on the knee and she yelled in pain and went down. I was horrified, and ran all the way home and hid in a closet.

I remained hidden until Dad came home and I heard him ask for me. I came out of the closet to face the music. He told me he knew what I had done and had paid Mr. Martinez for Antonieta's medical treatment. I knew Mr. Martinez would kill me the next time he saw me. As my Dad walked away he said that Mr. Martinez had said that next time I liked one of his daughters, to tell her, not to throw a stone in her direction. My Dad had a smirk or grin on his face.

I was glad that we moved back to Centerville but this time we went to live close to Alviso School at the Ted Murakami Farm. Here at Murakami Farms we lived behind Ted (*Chapo*) Murakami's home. He lived facing the highway and his parents had a matching home next to him. He was a very nice man and his wife and three kids were very pleasant. Dad and Roberto would help him on the farm whenever they were off from their regular jobs. Dad worked regularly for Planeta Farms and Roberto worked for Hunts Cannery at Hayward.

Every Saturday Roberto would drive Mom to Decoto now known as Union City for groceries. Mom insisted on going to Cardenas Grocery Store, and even though they had higher prices than the Lucky Stores, Mom wanted to go there because they were Hispanics. Mr. Cardenas would also offer credit when things were bad and that meant a lot to Mom, even though she would not use the credit. As soon as we got there I would open a coke and pour peanuts or corn nuts into it and start drinking. Mr. Cardenas would follow me like a store detective to see how much I would eat while in the store. When Mom was paying for the groceries he would always remind her that I had drank a soda and poured the peanuts into it. Mom would always pay for my damages, but I hated the store owner for being a tight wad and not looking the other way with my munchies.

When we ran short of something to eat Roberto and I would travel to Centerville to a grocery store there. One of the favorite things we bought there were chicken necks and backs. They were incredibly cheap and for a dollar we could buy about twenty pounds of them. Mom would make these cheap cuts into a feast and we would eat like hungry puppies until we could eat no more. The butchers at the Centerville store were Chinese and they caught on to our routine purchases and as we would near the meat department they would hold up a porterhouse steak knowing very well we would never buy one. As soon as we said we wanted a dollar of chicken necks and backs they would put the steak down and start to chant " Necks and backs, necks and backs". I hated them for it! I knew they were making fun of us because we were poor and could not afford the expensive meats. One thing we had plenty of and it was not cheap was family love. Our parents showed their love for us and we showed how much we loved them.

One day Dad was hurt at work and after several months of chiropractic treatments at Centerville it was diagnosed that his condition could only worsen if he continued to work irrigating the lettuce fields. Apparently he had pulled his leg joints out of their sockets. He decided that we would return to Mexico and think of some options. When Mr. Stivers found out that we were leaving and would probably not return, he asked me if he and his wife could adopt me. He scrambled Mr. Paulsen as an interpreter and went to visit my parents. Mr. Stivers told my parents that he was willing to send me to college and then I could return to them once I had been properly educated. I decided to stay with my parents and we returned to Mexico while I was in the eight grade.

After spending a few months at Sabinas, the decision was made for my Dad to remain in Mexico and work some lands the Mexican government had awarded him and others through a Land Act that had been passed. Mom, Lilia and I would return to Laredo, Texas and find a place to live while we attended school. We found an older home on Flores Street near Christen Middle School for me and McDonald Elementary School for Lilia.

I reported in to Christen Middle School and quickly made friends even thought this was not like California. At Alviso I had attended speech classes until my Spanish accent was eradicated and I spoke perfect English. Well, this seemed to bother some of my school mates and soon I was called a *"Gringo" lo*ver. Most of the school kids were great and I bothered only a few, unfortunately those carried knives and brass knuckles to school so they were a force to consider. The educational level was lower here so even thought I had missed several months of school time in the transfer from California, I was not behind.

In English, I was placed in Mr. Angel Cuellar's class and this was a high group. I met probably the best kids I was going to meet in Laredo in this 8th grade English. Mr. Cuellar was great with grammar and liked to give writing assignments. That was cool with me, besides he liked to talk about cooking different foods and that was O.K. with me also. Usually by the time he finished talking about different foods we were ready to eat a dinosaur. He was a Graduate of Texas A&M University and he wanted to prepare us to attend a school like that one. Even thought I did not attend Texas A &M University our son Mark did.

Juan Garza was the first boy I met at Christen and he talked about joining the Navy at all times. Then I met the gang that consisted of a group of football players. There was a nerdy but athletic boy named Reynaldo Godines who already had a nickname of "Comino" (Cumin Seed) because of his shape. There were other nerdy guys like Edmundo Ramirez, Steven (Roddy) Applewhite, Juvenal Herrera, and Roberto Rios. Then there were the diplomatic and nerdy ones such as Miguel Conchas, Gilbert Cardenas, Juan Cisneros, Carlos Carranco, and Quentin Vargas.

There were other boys that were very nice and did well in school or athletics. These boys like Tony Gonzalez, Juan Gutierrez, Joe Garza, Ernest Alvarado, David Duncan, Donato Martinez, Robert Brewster, Jose Luis Romero and Johnny Mejia were the hub of the class. They were involved in the sports and academic activities that made school fun. There were numerous other good boys that were doing well in school. I was not used to going to such a large school.

I had not experienced the organized sports environment, but before long I was in spring training with the football team. A boy named Pete Huizar convinced me to join. It was unusually hot in Laredo and getting acclimatized was difficult. All the football drills were fun with the exception of the somersaults. I just could not land on my feet after doing these exercises. With the exception of Mr.Paulsen at Alviso School I had never had a coach.

All of a sudden I was confronted with several coaches but the head coach was Dario Hinojosa. He had been a legendary athlete in Laredo and was well liked by the players and other coaches. John Silva, Eusevio (Chevo) Contreras and Andy Santos were his assistants and between the four they could run us raggedy. Andy Santos had been a member of the only Laredo basketball team to win a state championship. Contreras had been chosen to the High School All-American Team in baseball and earned an athletic scholarship to Texas University. I was surrounded by men who expected results but I was not used to all the yelling and the running around. It seemed we ran wind sprints and did pushups for everything. It was confusing! Before I really knew what was going on I found myself practicing for offensive guard.

Summer came and I went on to Sabinas to help Dad in a ranch he was developing. It was hot! I was not used to it since the summers in California were beautiful. Dad would work hard every day and his only break was to drive to Sabinas for supplies and to visit Mom and Lilia. I would help him in everyway I could such as digging holes for fence posts, hammering the nails to the posts to hold up the wire fence. The biggest chore was milking of the goats. Dad had purchased a herd of several hundred goats and he and the herdsman would milk them in the morning and in the evening.

The milk would be picked up by a milkman every morning and taken to Sabinas for processing into milk products, mostly cheese. Goat milk is very thick and creamy and very good for making cheese. When dad was helping the herdsman with the goats I would turn the milk over to the milkman. Sometimes on Sunday I would ride the milk truck into town and spend the day by going to the movies and eating junk food. Sometimes I was not ready to go and after the milk truck left I walked several miles to the Pan American Highway and hitched a bus into town. This was not my favorite option since I had the walk and cope with the heat, and also the commercial buses charged for the ride. Either way I had to pay on the way back and make the walk back to Dad's ranch.

During the day I made something to eat for Dad and I since the herdsman would only eat in the morning and at night. The morning meal consisted of eggs with dry beef (*machacado*) and pinto beans with flour tortillas and coffee. The noon meal was the lightest and consisted of either broiled *cabrito* (Baby goat) or of sardines and crackers. When we had *cabrito* at lunch we would usually have the rest of the goat at dinner time, since we did not have electricity at the ranch and therefore no refrigerator. When we went to town and brought fresh beef we would make it into dry beef (Jerky). It was hard living at the ranch since the only cold sodas or cold water was in town twenty miles away.

The summer was long and the conditions were primitive, but it helped me understand my father better, because this is how he had been raised. I had made a new friend in town named Rogelio Gomez . He was a smart boy who wanted to be a teacher. He combed his hair constantly.

He had seen Cookie Byrne in a movie and picked up the combing habit. He was very agile and played basketball very well.

I also met Juan and Cesar Montemayor two brothers who lived in the center of Sabinas and would spend the summers there. Later, I ran into them again at Martin High School in Laredo. I also met two other brothers Baldomero Garza and Jaime Garza who also attended school in Laredo but they attended Holding Institute which was a private school. These four guys were my friends then and are my friends today.

After the summer was over I returned to Laredo and attended the ninth grade at Christen Jr. High. I started playing football and somehow earned a starting position as guard. The previous year the team had gone undefeated and the coaches had expectations of another great season. The offensive line was composed of Ricardo Lopez and Juan Gonzalez at ends, Juan Gutierrez and Mario Alardin at tackles, Juvenal Herrera and I at guards and a boy named Jose P. Ramirez at center.

The halfbacks were Gilbert Negrete and Tony Gonzalez and the quarterback most of the time was Reynaldo Godines who also alternated with Jose Luis Romero. I say most of the time because Tony and Reynaldo would alternate at quarterback and halfback to confuse the opposing defenses and sometimes they confused us too. The fullback was whom ever the coach was not mad at the time of the game. Tony and Reynaldo did well scoring on the opposing teams and picked up the title of the "Touchdown Twins". My old friend from the neighbor hood Indalecio (Andy) Sada was also on the team and it seemed that his guitar was everywhere Andy was.

Picture of Christen Jr. High football Team,
Hinojosa and Silva were the coaches.

The first game was against Hebbronville and one of the most memorable to me because after the game I found out I was one of the game heroes. The score was 8 to our 6 in their favor. But then we scored again and since we had gone for two points on both touchdowns and had not made it it was now 12 to 8. We kicked off to them and I played on that formation but the ball went to the opposite side of the field. I was the player farthest from the runner with the ball.

The runner made a beeline run toward the end zone and all our players were blocked and then it was him and I. I was running across the field and the runner was running straight down the sideline when all of a sudden I was right in front of him and we collided and went down in front of our bench. We tumbled and rolled and our players and the students in the bleachers were all screaming. I did not realize that the game had ended and we had won, yes the game had ended and if he had made it we would have lost.

Later I found out how important my tackling that player had been. Unfortunately the glory of an offensive lineman is very limited and the rest of the season went by quietly. Of the nine games of the season we won four and lost four with one tied. We were somehow declared City Champs with Lamar Jr. High in second and St. Joseph Academy third. During the football season Juvenal Herrera and I became god friends. He had picked up the nickname of "Bruni" because he was original from a small town near Laredo with that name.

After football I joined the basketball team. I thought I was really on a roll and my friend Edmundo Ramirez and I were probably the worst players on the team, but we were a total of eight players so everyone counted and Coach John Silva was making the best of a bad situation. We practiced hard but for me it was a tough situation since coordination was not my most prized abilities.

The night of the first game Edmundo and I also had a conflict that our choir banquet was that night and we were having a nice dinner at the Plaza Hotel and we did not want to miss out on the free meal. The music teacher was a real nice lady named Consuelo Lopez and she was very good to us. Her husband Gregorio was always helping her with our school projects and was always ready to give the boys fatherly advice. They made everything worthwhile and meaningful to us.

Without telling Coach Silva we went to the choir banquet and had a great time. They had some high school girls singing to us and then of course the great meal. As we walked home from the banquet we were wondering what we would tell our coach. As we walked into the practice session what we heard from Coach Silva was not fitted to repeat in public. The coach's tone of voice was not friendly and we quickly surmised that we had been booted from the team and athletics for the rest of the year. So my basketball career or adventure was short lived.

The summer break came and I decided that this summer I would go work in the California farms. My brother Gregorio was in Hayward, California and made arrangements for me to travel to California with a friend of his from Sabinas named Luis Garza. I was to pay $20.00 dollars for my passage and go with a group of seven other men to California. It was somewhat crowded in the Ford station wagon with all the passengers and our clothes. There was no air condition in the car and it got pretty hot.

I was the only person in the load that could speak English and soon it became important. We had travel west toward California and the first night we had traveled nonstop to a place near Yuma, Arizona. Suddenly we were stopped by a parade of law enforcement officers at a road block. They dragged us out of the station wagon and pushed us against the car as they covered us with shotguns and other weapons. I heard one of the officers say "We got all the seven escapees but who's the kid they have".

The officers continued to celebrate their great apprehension when I found my tongue and told one of the officers that we were migrant workers going to California. He stopped the joyous celebration and informed the others what I had said. Suddenly everyone was quiet as they analyzed what I had said, most of them in complete disbelief. Finally they seemed to believe me and let us go. I did not think much of the situation but the other men who had been pushed around and had been scared out of their wits thought I had done a very brave thing, and suddenly I was like their kid hero.

Every stop we made, one of the men would buy me food or a drink. When we arrived in Pleasanton California at our work site the seven made a cooking and cleaning schedule and since they were seven, each one got a day of the week, except me. I became their interpreter and would help them buy the groceries which the cost was split by seven and I did not pay my share. I became a valuable member of the group.

The work in Pleasanton was hard as we worked hoeing in the fields all day long. It was very hot and humid and the only break from the boring and strenuous labor was an occasional water break. Occasionally the farmer would come and check on us, but for the most part we were left alone since we were expected to do our work and do it right. Hoeing weeds in the fields did not take a rocket scientist or someone with an engineering degree.

After a few weeks I left Pleasanton and went to work at a farm near Alvarado and to live with my sister Ofelia in Decoto. My sister was married to Carlos Juarez from Big Wells and they had two little girls, Nora and Nelda. My brother Gregorio lived near my sister's house and he and Elva had two little girls also, Norma and Nelly. My brother and brother-in-law both worked at Hunt's cannery in Hayward. I used Gregorio's Chevrolet Sport Coupe to go to work at the farm in Alvarado.

Soon, I was accepted well at the farm since I spoke English and was very punctual in attending work. I was trained to work with a tractor and therefore the work was easier for me. The hours were long and usually I worked twelve hours a day. I remember going to work with a light jacket because it was cold in the morning and then peeling all my clothes off except my pants since it got so hot around noon, but by the end of the day I was scrambling to get the jacket back on. Every day I would go by Johnny's Tachela's farm but I never got to see him, perhaps he was helping his father on their farm.

The summer months went by fast and very enjoyable because the weather was beautiful in central California. I saved my money to have spending money during the school year back in Laredo. Even though I was there the entire summer vacation the only friend from Alviso I saw was a girl named Sheila Newcomb. She was walking one afternoon holding hands with a young man in a subdivision near Alviso School. She never noticed me as she and the young man were talking and giggling.

CHAPTER 5

Good Times at Martin High

Soon, it was time to return to Laredo and attend school. I rode the bus on the return trip and although boring, it was safe. I arrived in Laredo just in time to register for the school year. My mother and sister Lilia joined me as they had spent the summer at Sabinas. Lilia was to attend McDonald Elementary and I was to attend Martin High School.

High school was a shocker to me. So many boys and girls and the school was so big. Mother reminded me that I was the first to reach high school and had to excel. I did not have the heart to tell her that we could not afford for me to attend college.

This was my sophomore year and the school subjects were harder than at the middle school. There were new subjects like typing with Miss Fasci and she was very strict so I took it again, oh no, not with her again. There was Chemistry with Miss Palacios and boy was she a hard teacher, and the material was not that easy to digest but somehow, we got thru it. That course was especially hard since someone had discovered how to make stink bombs. It was like going to school to smell spoiled hard boiled eggs.

There was Algebra with Angie Garcia and all you had to do was look at her and that was stimulant enough to do it. She would not show you how nice she really was so that you would try harder. There was government with Mrs. Kate Andrews who would read us letters from her son, who was serving in the Armed Services, and she would read them with so much pride in her voice we knew that it meant a lot to her. Then she would have us recite the Preamble to the Constitution daily and to this date I can still recite it. Thank you Mrs. Andrews, because as I grew, I realized what a great document it was and what it really meant. I also learned to love this country enough to want to protect what it stands for.

Then there was Kael Gonzalez government teacher, who would shake your hand with his huge hand and then he would squeeze yours, it made you think twice about wanting to shake hands with him. Mr. Lang was our Civics teacher and one of the projects was to take us to a real court environment. When we were there I was chosen to be Student Jury President. First we had to wait because the defense attorney was a recent law school graduate and this was his first trial, so they presented him with a reef. That young attorney named Julio Garcia gave it his best shot, which made the trial very interesting.

I ran into other teachers that I had had either in the eight grade or ninth grades at Christen Jr. High. Those teachers were Mr. Rodolfo Ibarra and Mr. Angel Cuellar who had followed us to the high school level. They taught the same subjects but at the higher pace. Then there was Mr. Francisco Peña at the science department and Mr. Fernando Macias in Algebra and Trig who were great role models for us.

I also took Science with Miss Ella Montemayor who was a very hard teacher but she would assign a science project to help out with our grade. A classmate (David Siegfried) decided he needed a good grade so he asked the teacher if he could prepare an owl for taxidermy. The teacher agreed and would ask David to bring the owl in to see how he was doing. David would bring the owl in a grocery bag and it seemed to us the only progress was that that owl was getting raunchier and it smell worse every time he brought it in. I personally don't think he finished processing the owl but it was a relief when he quit bringing it to school.

I reported to the football team and surprise, surprise, it seemed we had inherited the same coaches from the 9th grade. Now they seemed to yell a little louder. They expected more from us and now there were more of us since our old enemies from Lamar Jr. High were our teammates.

Now we were together since Martin High was the only public high school in Laredo at that time.

We inherited some good runners to augment the ones we had had at Christen Jr. High. We picked up a very athletic runner named Arturo Davalos, another very good runner named Richard "Dickie" Johnson and a big bruiser fullback named John Chamberlain. Davalos was also a good boxer while Johnson and Chamberlain were cowboys for the most part. Trying to bring Chamberlain down was like trying to bring down a big beef master bull. Nick Villarreal also joined us and even though he was sort of short in height he was tall in talent. We also acquired Hector Rocha at runner position, and Danny Guerrero, who would fill in as linebacker.

One day on the way to Pawnee the coached stopped the bus at George West to make reservations for our after the game meal. Some of us looked forward to that meal as it was probably the only restaurant meal we would have all week. We proceeded to Pawnee in early afternoon since the game was right after school hours. When we arrived, the looker room which was next to the football field was covered with black beetle bugs.

We received and were not able to move the ball. We figured that their players would eventually get tired since they only had ten players and had to play on both sides of the ball playing both offense and defense so we stayed calm even when the coaches were yelling at us very loud. Soon their pass catching end was hurt and they went to nine players. Their coach approached our bench and again asked to forfeit the game. Our coaches were now furious and said "No" so the game continued with them playing only nine players.

Well when the game ended it was 33-0 in their favor. Coach Hinojosa who was a pretty dark fellow was now purple and what was coming out of his mouth was not church talk. I had never seen our coaches this mad. Our return trip was like a funeral procession. Even John Chamberlain and Dickie Johnson who were always playing tricks on everyone from the back of the bus were very quite. Old Henry the bus driver was acting as if he was in mourning. Finally we arrived at George West and I could hardly wait for the chicken fried steak and mash potatoes. As the bus stopped and we started to rush the door

Coach Hinojosa stood up and blocked the exit and said "You guys don't deserve to eat, so sit down".

He got off the bus and paid the restaurant for the meal we did not eat and we left back to Laredo. It was a long trip back because we were so hungry we could not sleep. Sometimes when I got to bed hungry I remember that evening. We knew that the following week would be a long one on the practice field. The Pawnee game was not the only game we were ridiculed.

One day we traveled to D'hanis, Texas and as we approached the very small populated area and we saw how small the town was it was we knew it was time to beware. Like in Pawnee most of the football players came from the surrounding ranches and farms and they were pretty strong. Trying to block their defensive linemen was a tough job. For me weighting in at one hundred and forty pounds trying to block a three hundred pound middle linebacker was almost impossible.

On one series of downs the middle linebacker knocked me into the quarterback Reynaldo Godines and sacked him. The next couple of downs were a replica of the first and Godines was losing his composure. Actually, he was very mad, mad enough to throw the football at me and hit me in the groin. I carried that grudge for more than thirty years but I got even with him. One day as he operated on me I came out of the anesthesia and smacked him in the face, put that in your medical book Dr. Godines. Well, the game was off to a bad start as the score at the end of that game was in the forties for them and zero for us.

Things in school were hectic and with all the new activities at the school and the long homework assignments and then practice after school, well it was mind boggling. One day after practice Robert Brewster and I walked across the street to get a soda before going home. The drive in store was across the football field and the sodas were very reasonable. We bought our usual Nehi fruit drinks and sat on a bench in front of the store to drink them so we could return the bottles. There were two young girls minding the store and before long they were talking to us about school and the football team. One of the girls was named Elsa Garza and the other was Linda Pruneda. Well six years later Linda and I were married and forty years after that we are still married. It must have been a big soda that I purchased that afternoon.

The football season got somewhat better when we started to play the small schools around Laredo such as Mirando City and Bruni. The varsity team was doing real well and of course the coaches would rub it in. The varsity team had a big offensive and defensive line with guys like Jerome Czar, Jesse Garcia, Victor Woods, Francisco Ibarra, John Spruill, Chester Long, Ray Alvarez and Chuck Richter.

These guys were not only big young men they were very athletic. The quarterbacks were Agustin Luna as starter and David Sauceda and Gabriel Palacios as backups, The fullback was Victor Alcocer with Rodolfo Rios and George Haynes at halfbacks The varsity team won eight of the ten games and lost only two. The two games they lost were to Hardendale and Brackenridge, both San Antonio schools.

Brackenridge had a runner named Warren McVea who would go on to the Pros if that is an indication of how good an athlete he was. Both of those losses were very memorable to us in the JV because the varsity line coach Glen Woods would make us stand with the ball over our heads and have the varsity players tackle us at full speed. Yes, they would tackle us as if we were the ones who had lost. That part of the game of football I never understood and coach Woods, well you could say I hated him.

The junior year came upon us fast and the big players moved on to colleges and several played in the semi pros. Martin High School was not the only high school in town because now they had opened Nixon High School across town to the east. Now we were faced with a dilemma that of the only seven returning lettermen they were divided and three lettermen went on to attend Nixon leaving four lettermen in Martin. It was going to be hard to equal or beat the previous year's record.

There was a bit of good news with the opening of the new high school Coach Woods had moved to Nixon. (And don't come back, you hear.) Coach Calvin Voekel remained as head coach at Martin, while Calvin Hustler, Danny Villarreal, Dario Hinojosa, Chevo Contreras, Andy Santos and Albert Ochoa were the assistants. The trainer was a great gentleman by the name Luis Novoa and the team doctor was Dr. Leo Cigarroa. We knew that it was going to be tuff and we were not wrong.

We had Conrado Hein and Rey Godines at quarterback. We managed to beat two teams, but both were first year schools, one was Kennedy in San Antonio and the other was our cross town rival Nixon.

The other eight teams we played beat us as we headed for one of the worst school records in Martin's history. There were some worst years later but those can't be blamed on us. Beating Nixon even though they had been our friends the year before was very satisfying and beating Coach Woods was simply great.

Picture of some of us playing Donkey Basketball,
and some of the cheerleaders.

During the Nixon game which was the last one of the season I got a small chance to play for Benny Salinas one of the starters toward the end of the game. I went in for the left end and Conrado Hein our quarterback called for a down and out, which meant I would go about ten yards straight down and then turn toward the side lines. I knew he would not throw me the pass so instead I cut toward the inside which put me in close pattern with Nino Rodriguez the right end and in competition for the ball. Well, Conrado was being pressured in the backfield and fired the ball and I grabbed it and headed for the end zone.

Well, soon after I got the ball I felt a pain in my rib cage and the lights went out and at the same time the crowd roared. I guessed that I had scored a touchdown, but soon found out that Ruben Vela the

Nixon Safety had hit me hard with his helmet and that's why I thought the lights had gone out. In reality I had run for over thirty yards but the game was over and I had not scored the touchdown. The only good thing was that no one made fun at me because we had won anyway with the score of 24-8.

After each home game we would have record hops at the gym and we danced our problems away. After the Nixon game the festivities and the dance were very enjoyable. Since now I was a junior and I was not a starter, next year I would have to improve or do something else like work after school and on weekends. Yes, I had to do something because the competition was going to be tough. So I started planning for the following year by inquiring what kind of programs were available my senior year. I decided that I would get into a program called Distributive Education or DE.

The Distributive Education Program was run by one of my old junior high teachers Mr. Carlos Carranco. After talking to him it seemed that he would accept me into the program. He explained to me that there would be no room on my time schedule to participate in football and I agreed. That was probably the best course for me to take. I would drop football and join Distributive Education since I was going to work part of the day in some business and within the down town area or some kind of entity there would be no time to practice and play football.

So meanwhile I continued being a junior in high school and enjoying the added activities that came along with being a junior. I searched for a part-time job and I ended up working at the little store across the high school where I had met Linda. It seems that the store was owned by her parents and I was able to work part-time and very conveniently go to school since it was just across the street. Meanwhile the romance with Linda continued. We would go to the school activities together. We would attend record hops and other events liked by George Washington Parade which at that time and even now is one of the biggest activities in Laredo.

So summer came and I had to search for a real job and the one that will provide funds for the oncoming year for clothes and school activities etc. etc. I decided to travel to Fort Wayne Indiana, where my brother Roberto and his new bride Mayra were living. There I would work during the summer months before returning to Martin High School my senior year. I traveled by bus to Fort Wayne Indiana and join my brother and his wife where they lived in a very nice and comfortable apartment at 2911 Weiser Park. They made me feel very welcome.

My brother took me to his place of employment which was a business called Art Mosaic and it was a construction company where they specialized in tile and terrazzo floors. They did a lot of school work, restaurants, and big businesses. There I was hired as a laborer at $2.50 an hour, which was outrageously high for me. The foreman was an Italian gentleman by the name of Pete and he took me to their warehouse where they were unloading sacks of marble granite and cement sacks from these railroad cars onto the warehouse storage area and then reloaded them onto trucks to go to the worksites as needed. It was hard work for a high school junior that weighed one hundred and forty pounds to move granite bags weighting one hundred and twenty pounds of granite.

Somehow, I survived and competed with the college football players from Purdue and Indiana Universities that were working there to stay in good shape. I was impressed by the other workers because they were so strong and I guess they had to be since they were college lineman etc. and trying to keep up with them was a little hard. They could toss the hundred and twenty pound bags from one to the other as they joked and laughed and while I grunted and sweated. Soon the foreman came and decided to move me to an outside job working where they were installing to terrazzo floors. There were only two jobs I could do there, either mix materials or carry the materials to the masons in buckets.

The work crew was made up two older gentlemen by the name of Eugene and his son-in-law Angelo. The two helpers would assist the two men. Well, there were actually three helpers. There was Angelo's son Renato and me ferrying the materials to the two older men and there was a relative of mine named Armando who ran the mixer.

Eugene and Angelo who were the masters of the trade with the granite floors and would work harmoniously during the day until tempers would flare. When these tempers flared there wasn't a bad word in English or Italian that was not tossed about. So in a way it was like I was going to summer school and learning Italian. When they would go at each other, Angelo's son Renato and I were included in the verbal exchange. Sometimes these things would get so heated that they would waive their metal troughs at each other and I wondered if they were going to attack each other. Neither one made a step forward instead they attacked each other with another verbal barrage. Sometimes the son would join in and relaxed both his father and his grandfather as I looked a little bit in disbelief.

One of the buildings we were working on was an elementary school which I had attended years before back in the 50s and the place where I had eaten the little girl's lunch. I had to carry the terrazzo mixed with the cement up to the second and third floors on stairs that were not finished yet. One day after carrying the heavy buckets all day I was very tired and went home, sat by the TV and didn't take a shower or ate supper, before I knew it was time to get up and go to work again. The buckets had been so heavy I thought my hands were dragging on the ground. No matter how tired I was, it was just another work day at Art Mosaic. This company was not a work place for sissies.

And so the summer months passed and I continued working for Art Mosaic. I learned a lot of Italian (bad words) and saved a lot of money for the coming year. In the evenings and weekends my cousin Rupert and I would do a ride around and later go for a movie and ice cream. Then it was time to go back to Laredo and finish high school. This time I rode the train. From Fort Wayne the train took me to Indianapolis and then south to St. Louis and then straight to Laredo, Texas. Most of the times I rode on the upper levels because it is was more scenic and there was music in the background. Before I knew it I was in Laredo Texas again.

The school year started off with a bang. Since it was my senior year I had very few classes to take and I could participate in the Distributive Education Program known as DE. I would go to school till approximately 1 o'clock in the afternoon and then report to my work place downtown. I had to walk all away downtown and be there by two o'clock in the afternoon and that was including my lunch break. In the morning I would have several classes especially one that I enjoyed probably the most about high school and that was Distributive Education. Mr. Carranco was no longer at Martin High School because now he was a school principal somewhere else. He had been transferred during the summer.

At first I thought I was not going to enjoy this class because now we had a new teacher and he was very nice but very strict. At that time I didn't know that the new teacher, Mr. Rogelio Salinas was going to have such an influence on me. This man had a different style but once he established himself he was a very nice person. I didn't know that this teacher was going to make me excel in that Distributive Education Program. He was very soft-spoken yet he had such influence in his voice in every activity we did that you couldn't help but listen to the man. His wife and daughters were always part of the program and that made us feel as if we part of his family.

My workstation was to be JC Penney in downtown Laredo. I reported to JC Penney and was introduced to Mr. Pagel who was the store manager and Mr. Payne who was the assistant store manager. I was advised that my workstation would be the stockroom because JC Penney did not allow students to be on the sales floor. I accepted my job and went upstairs to the stockroom to meet my coworkers. The manager of the stockroom was a man named Pablo Vasquez and his assistant was a man named Sixto. Pablo was very strict with us and he rarely smiled but inside he was a very nice person. There were two young girls named Marta Guerrero and Rosario Botello marking all the clothes and linen, but they rarely spoke and all day they just did their work. Two other men also worked there ferrying the merchandise down to the three sales floors.

Working in the stockroom was hard work yet you could make it into fun if you wanted to. The stockroom was on the third floor and had an old cranky elevator but I preferred the stairs. When one of the salesmen or salesladies needed something I would grab it and run down the stairs and delivered and run upstairs and back to work. This activity kept me in wonderful shape and I didn't miss football.

I was scheduled to work 20 hours because I was a student and I would be paid $.92 an hour however if I went over 20 that was considered overtime and I would be paid the regular employee wage of a $1.25. I always tried to work the 40 hours so that I would get the extra money to help out at home and have some change for myself.

The hardest job in J.C. Penney was to mop and re-wax the floors which was done by the persons assigned to the stockroom except for the women which were the girls Marta and Rosario. When it was wax day no one was told until the last minute so that no one skipped out on the duty. All of a sudden we were told that the floors had to be done and the job usually ended around midnight.

When we had to clean the floors I was not allowed to go home until the work was done whether I had homework or not didn't matter but I could not advise my mother of where I was because we didn't have a telephone and sure enough as soon as it got dark my mother would come looking for me at the store and she would stand by the door until she would see me go by with the mop or mop bucket. She would go home now that she knew that I was safe. That week the check was very nice because of the extra hours.

One day I asked my father if I could have a car since this was my senior year. His response was that when I was ready to let him know and he would make a trip from Sabinas and we would look for a car. I quickly said that I was ready now, and he asked if I had the money to pay for it. I said no, and he quickly said that I was not ready.

One day as I walked to Martin High, I spotted a black 1954 Ford for sale. I rang the door bell and the owner was an airman and he wanted one hundred and fifty dollars for the car. The car ran well and was automatic but the interior was completely sheared to pieces and the man sat on a board when he went to work. He explained that he had left his collie in the car while they shopped and the dog went berserk and tore all the upholstery down to the metal springs.

Now, I had to save the money and call my Dad. I stopped to see the car when it was down to one hundred dollars as the airman had gotten orders to ship out and he took my life's savings for the car. Dad came from Mexico and we closed on the deal. I was so proud of my black Ford and it didn't matter that I had to sit on a board to keep the springs from tearing my pants. Soon I saved fifty-five dollars and had the car upholstered in Mexico. And now it was red and white inside. Wow! I had status now. But I also had expenses like gas and oil, and tires. One evening I had two flats and had to walk home.

The senior year went by very fast. There were all the activities we had to participate in. I was informed that I had been selected as runner-up for Most Handsome Senior Boy. Soon after that I was selected as the King of the Senior Prom.

The year was coming to a close and I was also busy competing in the events with the Distributive Education Program. I had decided to compete in Sales Demonstration. We traveled to San Antonio, Texas where the Area Competition was being held at Holmes High School. I was a bit nervous but it seemed to me that everyone else was too.

I was to demonstrate a set of sports slacks and a sport coat to a prospective buyer. I was on the stage when the buyer walked on to the stage. I had taken average sizes and he was about five feet tall and very petite. I knew that I had to act and act fast or the competition was going to be over. I greeted him and started to tell him about our new line of sports clothes and asked him to try them on. As soon as he put the oversized sport coat I new I was in trouble. He looked like when a child puts on his daddy's clothes to look like him. He looked ridiculous. I had to save the day, so I commented loudly so that everyone in the auditorium could hear. "Wow. A perfect fit and on the first try". There was a small pause and the entire crowd started laughing and clapping. Then they stood up and continued to clap. I darted a quick glance at Mr. Salinas and he was smiling and clapping, and to me that was enough, after all he was my mentor.

The competition continued and I was not surprised when I placed first. Placing first meant I would go on to State Competition in Dallas. And as the preparations started for the State Competition I wondered how I would do in the much harder competition.

The day finally came and we headed for Dallas. The convention hall where I had to compete was jammed packed with students parents and spectators. This time I had no rabbit to pull out of a hat. It was just hard competition with all the schools trying to take the state honors home. I was not going to let Martin High School down, especially Mr. Salinas. The top three places were considered as All-Stators and when the smoked cleared I had placed second. Again Mr. Salinas was delighted by my accomplishments. I came home feeling proud of what I had achieved.

What could I do next now that I was on a roll. I had heard that some students were being named as High School All-Americans and I wondered. About that time I received a letter from the President of the United States and again my head ballooned. Could I have been considered for All American status? I did not open the letter instead I placed it in a book and took it to school. In the hall way I met Mrs. Kate

Andrews who had been my government teacher and told her about the letter from the President and she was a bit shaken and said "Oh my".

Mrs. Andrews quickly read the letter and then asked me to read it. It began with "Dear Victor, this is from the Office of the President of the United States of America Lyndon B. Johnson. You are herby inducted into the Armed Forces of the United States" Boy! I was drafted into the military just like that. But I was still in High School and had plans to attend Indiana University.

My stomach went sour and I had this sick feeling. What a dreamer I was thinking one thing and ignoring the obvious. I had heard in the news that the Army was having a tuff time in Viet-Nam. The Army's 1st Cavalry Division had been involved in a big battle and they had killed thousands of enemy soldiers however they had losses too. I did not want to think that I was going to war straight from high school.

Graduation was coming and we would see what would happen. Maybe I could beat the draft although that did not seemed likely. The Senior Prom arrived and I did my thing crowning the Queen and enjoyed the dance. While all the other seniors rented fancy cars to go to the prom, I rode in my black 1954 Ford. I did not have to pretend, after all I was taking the prettiest girl I knew to the prom.

There were a lot of dances and record hops to attend. We went to dances with Sunny and the Sunliners, Jimmy Edwards and Latin breed, Little Joe and Johnny and the Latineers, The Royal Jesters and others. (Ironically on Aug.7, 2009, some forty five yeas later we attended a birthday party function by Sunny and the Sunliners and Little Joe and the Familia for Webb County Judge Danny Valdez.).

We also had our own local music heroes the Quarter Notes which were four young men, Rene Herrera, Rene Ornelas, John Orfila, and Juan Garza-Gongora. These guys could really sing well, and soon Rene and Rene were on their own and even sang on Dick Clarks' American Bandstand with their hit song *Angelito*". There were other upcoming groups called the Rondels, and another group called the Peppers that were doing real well.

Well, the day that I had been waiting for came and I graduated from high school Linda's parents gave me a graduation and farewell party at the same time since the next morning bright and early I left to work in Fort Wayne, Indiana. While everyone else was still celebrating the graduation with parties I was on a Greyhound Bus headed north.

I arrived safe and sound on Sunday night and Monday morning was back at Art Mosaic working. Pete the foreman assigned me as a helper with my cousin Pete Treviño who was a tile setter for the company. Pete and his wife Janice had a baby girl named Laura and that was Pete's pride and joy. We mostly worked the surrounding towns near Ft. Wayne and we worked by ourselves. Pete was established in his routine setting tile and did not require anyone looking over his shoulders. He knew what to do and did it.

We got along very well as I would prepare the mixture Pete needed to set his quarry tile and he did the rest. In the morning he would pick me up in his fairly new Chevrolet red and white sport coupe. I slept all the way to the work site and on the return trip I drove while he napped. He never asked me if I had a driver's license and I never told him I did not.

On Saturdays Pete had a Spanish radio show there in Fort Wayne. The Treviño Brothers had also purchased a dance hall in Holgate, Ohio named the Swiss Gardens. At the Gardens they would host Mexican bands for dances. The Swiss Gardens included a home on the property and a restaurant and apartment inside the dance hall. I met several Latino bands there as they played usually for several weeks at the Swiss.

Soon I applied for work at General Motors at Defiance, Ohio. It was a plant that produced engine blocks so the work was hard, mostly foundry type. I had moved to Defiance and lived with my brother Gregorio and his wife Elva. It was about fifty miles from Ft. Wayne and not having a car was hard to attend work. The Swiss was nearby in Holgate and I could help out on weekends there. The Treviños were going places and I felt good being around them.

I was hired at GM and started to work the next day. I loved it there even though the work was challenging. They had a very nice cafeteria for the employees and the food was excellent, and being a chow hound, well that meant a lot to me. My first job was to work on the V-8 assembly motor pouring line. I was happy here and my brother Gregorio, and cousin Jose Angel Treviño also worked there.

There on the line we assembled the sand cores for the engines before they were poured with hot metal. The line went by pretty fast and I had to place these spacers that kept the larger sand molds separated. The older more experienced employees kept me from making a mistake. Every mistake would cause an engine block from being poured perfect and would be put aside.

Soon my supervisor a red headed engineer named Mr. Young came by, looked at me and asked me if I wanted to transfer to the sand mixers. I said yes, and he took me to my new job. It consisted of overseeing two types of sand being mixed for the engine cores. The moisture and texture of the sand had to be just right for the molds to hold when they were poured with the hot melted iron.

My job was to reach over when the sand was going by to the molds, and grab a sample and feel it out. If it did not feel just right I would alter the amount of hot sand with the amount of wet sand until it felt just right. About every fifteen minutes the lab people would come over and take a sample for the lab and post the results on the board so every one could see how the mixture was in consistency. Soon I was doing real well and the job was a breeze. I spent my time singing and walking in place. No one could see me, and they definitely could not hear me over the laud noise of the machinery.

I loved my job and the summer months went by fast. One day Mr. Young the Engineer Supervisor came by and told me that every one was happy with my performance and there was talk about sending me to Indiana Tech to be an Engineer and then have a contract with GM. This was good news even if Mr. Young was not serious.

One day, I received a reminder that I had been inducted and to report on Sept. 26, 1966 to the Armed Forces Station at Indianapolis, Indiana. I showed the letter to Mr. Young and he was real serious and told me "Vic, you are a hot potato, there is no way I can save you". From that day on the summer went by faster. Soon it was time to report in, so I resigned my job at General Motors and said goodbye to the workers on the assembly line. I said my goodbyes to my brothers and their wives and the Treviños. The Treviños were doing well with their radio shows and their Swiss Garden. Ruperto Jr. was setting the pace by getting ready to go to Engineer School at Purdue.

As I left for the Army one man at the plant reminded me not to volunteer for anything.

CHAPTER 6

I'm in the Army Now

I left by bus from Ft. Wayne to Indianapolis the state Capital. There in Indianapolis I went straight to the Induction Center. It was full of new recruits. There were the ones that volunteered and those that had been drafted. It was hectic with all those new faces inquiring about what they were headed for. There were forms to fill out but the most important was the physical which was performed by real professionals (these guys were professional rubber stampers).

Once you got in front of them you were going in. The boy that was in front of me, had a birth deformity in that one rib cage was like caved in. The so called doctor approved him for service and told him to proceed with his processing. When I was next I pointed to the doctor what I could see from just being in line in back of the young man. The doctor yelled "Hey, dummy, get out of line and process out".

I went to lunch at the local YMCA which was near the Induction Center. I grabbed my tray and was served some food and when I finished started to walk away when this man started to yell at me all kinds of crap. It seemed that he wanted me to pick up the tray, scrape the food and place the tray in the wash room. He could have explained to me what he wanted, instead he yelled at me to entertain the other people eating. Perhaps this was an army general or someone that wanted to be a general. I knew I would never forget that idiot!

I returned to the station only to be placed in a formation by height.

We were told that if we were taller than the man in front to tap him on the shoulder. This went on in several directions until the tallest guys were in the front three rows. I was on the fourth. At that time a Marine Corps Drill Sergeant appeared and spoke to us in a Marine Corps manner.

"Gentlemen, due to the heavy losses the Marines have suffered in Viet-Nam these past few months the Marines are now inducting men into service. The first three rows of men have just been selected to be Marines". The groaning could be heard through out the large room. Wow! That was close, and thanks to the tall young men in our group. Yes, if things had been different I would have gone to the Marines, but thanks to being a six foot shorty, I was not.

Within minutes it seemed we were on a bus on the way to Fort Leonard Wood, Missouri, and on our way to an adventure in the U. S. Army. We traveled by night and in the very early hours of the next day we arrived at the fort near the Ozarks. It was Sept 27, 1966 a date that I would remember better than December 7th 1941. Not because there would be infamy with the date, but my life would change forever. Even though I did not know it at that time, it would change for the better, I just had to get through some obstacles first.

We were now at the fort and we hungry. The bus unloaded us at the Reception Station and a couple of polite Drill Sergeants received us and marched us to the mess hall. Before we were allowed to eat we had to do chin-ups outside the mess-hall. After eating the green looking scrambled eggs, the bacon that smelled like a real pig, the cold burnt toast and washed it down with the strongest coffee I had ever tasted, we were walked on line back to the Reception Station. All the time we were walking back we were looking for cigarette buts and other trash. This was called police call. I had a problem with this, first it was too dark to see anything and second I had not thrown the butts or the trash. This meant someone could throw trash and some one else was responsible for picking it up, something was not right here.

Finally, the sun came up and we could see each other. I had a new haircut when I got there but some of the guys had real long or bushy hairy, after all this was the sixties. We were taken into the Reception Station and forms had to be filled out and then there were shots to be taken. I was scared of needles but these were like pressure guns that gave us our shots. We were in real close to the guy in front and back. Someone kept yelling "Make you buddy smile" what ever that meant. I was so close to the other guys that when they gave me a shot I fainted and I took down about five other guys.

Now it was time to go eat again, except now doing the pull ups hurt because of the shots. The Drill Sergeants kept yelling for everything, it seemed they could not talk, just yell for everything. The food was much better and we were not half-asleep so we could see it. There was roast beef and potatoes and lots of gravy, also there was corn and green beans and desert but no *tortillas* There was always cold milk or fruit punch. Then there was walking back on line and looking for the trash someone else had thrown.

We got back to the Reception Station and there were more forms to fill out and a trip to the barber shop. We were now marched to the barber shop where they had four samples on the wall of how you wanted your hair. I told them I did not need a haircut as I had gotten one in Ft. Wayne, I was quickly told to shut up and get in line as I was going to get one anyway. Would you believe they took all my beautiful hair completely off. One guy that had a big mole in the middle of his head covered by a large red afro, well the mole came off also and they had to rush him to the hospital to stop the bleeding.

After the mess at the barber shop we were marched to what was going to be our home the rest of the week there at the Reception Station. It was several double-decker barracks with double bunks on both sides. We were issued our blankets a pillow and case. We were shown how to make our beds and then it was time to eat again. The chin up bar was first and then supper. Those metal trays made a lot of noise, but again the food was good and more of it. I could grow to like this place if only the Drill Sergeants would stop yelling.

After supper we were finally on our own. We could take showers, after all it had been more than two days since we had left home. But first we had to make a duty roster for fire patrol. Every hour one of us on each floor of the barracks had to walk around the floor patrolling for recruits going AWOL or for fires in the building and that the windows to the barracks stay open for two inches to prevent meningitis.

Everyone was ready to hit the sack. We curled in between the sheets and soon we were looking for the blankets as it cooled down in the late

September night. I did not get guard duty the first night so that was O.K. I was very tired and went to sleep right away. About midnight we were woken to the sounds of war! There was yelling and lots and machine gun fire real close to us. My god, were we at war already? Finally someone yelled out that we were close to the Infiltration Course, and that was all the noise. It was several hours later I finally went to sleep. Now it was time to get up again.

Now it was Wednesday and we started by doing pull ups and eating breakfast. The food never really changed but now we noticed there was oatmeal and grits. I tasted the grits and left them on the tray. The coffee was getting better but not great. Again we fanned out for the police call looking for those cigarette buts in the dark. Wouldn't it be easier to catch the guy that was doing this than to look for the buts every day after every meal. Maybe outlaw smoking on the base since some one could not keep from throwing the buts on the ground. Maybe it was to hard for the generals to figure it out, but after all if they had trained at the YMCA it should be easy for them, unless they were the ones smoking.

Well, we started off with shots again and this time I managed not to pass out. Just in case no one stood behind me. How many are they going to give us, I thought they have given us enough. Then we reported in for testing, which took all morning. It seemed to me they should have tested us before we entered the Service. Now, it was time for lunch and again the food was getting better, but the chin ups were getting harder. The Drill Sergeants kept on yelling but now it was getting louder.

When we reported back, I was one of the ones that got called out for counseling. First, the drill sergeant laughed at me when he announced that I had gotten a 13 percentile on mechanical and analytical. "Are you a real dummy, I have never seen such a low score" he yelled. I was unimpressed with his yelling since the day at the YMCA whoever yelled to me it meant the same thing. It seemed to me that all these people hollering had a low I.Q.

It seemed that I had done real well on the comprehensive exams and now qualified to take the Officer Candidate School Exam. They asked if I wanted to take it and I said yes, and passed it with good standings. I was told that now I was a candidate to attend Officers Candidate School. Now it was dinner time and pull ups again. One more police call and to the barracks. This time I drew the patrol duty but I was the first one on so the sacrifice of getting up in the middle of the night was not so hard. I dressed up with a helmet liner, flashlight and a military whistle to wake everyone in case of fire. The night passed without incident except for one of the guards stepping on a thump tack that some one threw in his path to show he did not have his shoes on.

The next day was Thursday and it was time to get uniforms. I had always been told that I had very large feet. I figured that when the Army did not have shoes for me they would send me home. After all I could not be in the service barefooted. They marched us to some place on post at a double time. Many recruits fell out and we had to wait for them at the Clothing Store. Once everyone was there we formed up to get our uniforms. First was a large green military bag to put our uniforms in and was called a duffel bag.

There was a soldier in front of me that was complaining that he wanted to go home. I told him not to worry because he had huge feet and was probably going home anyway because certainly the Army did not have such huge footwear. This seemed to cheer him up as he went on from station to station. When he got to the footwear he yelled 13.5 length, and three D in width. The civilian attendant threw him two pair of boots and a pair of low quarters. Boy, I was doomed with my 101/2 D size for footwear. Well, we went through all the stations and received green uniforms for the field and for dress and even some kakis for casual wear. We were issued several pair of gloves for field, dress and for the rifle ranges.

Now, it was time to go back to the barracks with our huge green bag of uniforms. I wondered if we would fit in a military bus with those huge bags. I did not have long to wonder as the Drill Sergeants formed us up in formation and started the trip back to the reception station, at a double time(run). There were recruits dropping out like flies, their large duffel bags dropping to the ground. I did not drop out but at times I wanted to. When we got back to the barracks there were less than one third of the ones that started the trek. We would remember that day for a long time. It took most of the day to get everyone together again. But the party was not over, since now we had to fold our uniforms, shine our boots and shoes etc.

Well, we had endured the first week of Army life. We had graduated from the reception station and were on our way to basic training. If someone asked me what I remember from the first week it would be the shots, the police call, the chin up bar, the yelling and the strong coffee. Oh, yes the machine gun firing and bomb blasts coming from the Infiltration Course.

CHAPTER 7

Basic Training

We were bussed over to our new home at company E, Second Battalion of the Third Training Brigade, across the post from the reception station. Our Commander was Capt Alfred A. Demarest and our training would start on October, 10 and end on December 1, 1966. Our Drill Sergeants would be SSG Avery and SSG Velez.

SSG. Avery was a big black man and SSG Velez was a short Puerto Rican and between both they would bring smoke upon us. First there was the drill and ceremonies or marching. And if it was not hard enough by ourselves they added the M-14 rifles to complicate matters. Of course there was the physical training, bayonets, obstacle course and rifle range to contend with. Also there was record range and target detection close combat and obstacle course. Then when you could march and shoot there was the gas chambers, hand to hand fighting, grenade throw, bayonet fighting and more.

At last there was the physical training which included the infamous monkey bars, the obstacle course, grenade throw, the run and the low crawl. And then the big daddy of it all, the Proficiency Test where you would be tested for everything else, like first aid, your general orders, your protection against chemical and biological agents. By now you knew how to wear your uniform, make your bed, detect targets and take your weapon apart and clean it. And don't forget the Infiltration Course where we had to low crawl with our rifle while they fired real

M-60 machine guns over our heads and simulated bombs were going off as we crawled. This was the ruckus we had heard at the reception station.

Every morning we practiced the monkey bars on the way to the mess hall and of course no one had caught the smoker so we had to do police call. It started to get cold and soon it was snowing. For the recruits from Minnesota it was a blessing, for a kid from Texas it was hell. SSG Velez kept telling us to make our bed properly every day. He said one day when you come of the rifle range you are going to find your bed at the bottom of the stairwell. We did not think he would do it but one day as we came into the barracks from the cold from being at the range all day there was a bunk, mattress, sheets, pillow and blankets at the bottom of the stairwell.

We all laughed and wondered whose bed it was. When I reached the bay where I lived with seven other soldiers, my corner was empty. Suddenly, I realized that was my bed downstairs and the joke was on me. I quickly retrieved my bed, made it and ran to supper through the snow.

I made only one good friend at Basic Training and that was Gary Martincic. We would go to Waynesville to the movies together. At that time Clint Eastwood was releasing his spaghetti westerns and we saw them all. It was fun going to Waynesville but it was a hazard to return to post late at night.

It was getting close to graduation from Basic Training. SSG Avery was pretty cool but SSG Velez kept yelling at me louder and louder. He would always say "Look me in the eye Speedy Gonzalez", which was the nickname he had given me. Finally one day I asked him why he was on me all the time? His reply was that I was being considered to go to OCS and had to show a little more than the others, besides he said "Your are Hispanic like me". I found it hard to look him in the eye since his head was crooked from a tank accident he had had early in his career.

CHAPTER 8

Advanced Individual Training

Well, we received our orders to go to Advanced Individual Training and I moved to the Old Hospital Area of the post. This was a ghostly building that had been built during the big wars to house the many wounded. It had barracks for the care givers which were our barracks and the long corridors that led to the old wards. Now the wards were used to train company clerks and other administration personnel. It had a huge Mess Hall and PX with Barber Shop within the building. There were so many corridors you could get lost. The Drill Instructors would march us down the corridors, and sometimes at a double time. The noise made on the wooden corridors was deafening. However, when it snowed going on the long corridors was simply wonderful.

Every day we would go to class in one classroom of what used to be a medical bay. The instructors were very good but being inside all day was not good. Soon we would be company clerks and personnel specialists. I was beginning to be a good typist because the Army stressed accuracy over speed. I only wished Miss Fasci could see me now, maybe she would be proud of me, (I said maybe).

We continued to do drill and ceremonies and physical training. Those we did outside in the snow, of course the recruits from the northern states loved it, but I did not. I think the activity I hated the most was buffing the floors in our barracks. Somehow balancing the buffer was not my bag.

We continued going to Waynesville to the movies and to grab an occasional pizza. The movies on post were not bad, there was a John Wayne series of recent release that was showing. We saw The Sons of Katie Elder, Rio Lobo, Rio Bravo and several more.

Well, it was time to graduate as fully trained administration clerks. Just as we graduated there was a world situation known as the Pueblo Crisis. We were all asked to pack our uniforms and get ready for shipment to Korea. There would be no leave of any kind and we would ship out in the early morning. I packed my bags and then stood in formation outside in the dark. It was raining and we were all wet as were our duffel bags.

After being outside for an hour and accounting for every member of the class the 1st SGT came out side and yelled out my name. He said for me to go back to the barracks and go to sleep, and he would deal with me later. I did as told and about morning and after everyone was shipped out he explained to me that I was not going to Korea because I was going to OCS.

As fast as you can blink an eye I was transferred to a holding company on the south side the post. There I would wait until I received orders for Officers Candidate School. I was quickly processed and told I had kitchen police (KP) the following week for an entire week. Well, I reported to the Mess Steward for detail. I was not the only one, actually there were five of us. I did not understand why if I was going to be a leader of men I had to do kitchen police. This sounded like doing police call when I did not smoke. By now I would have already caught the smoker and there would be no need for the police call.

The Mess Steward asked for a show of hands who knew how to peal potatoes. I remembered the man at GM telling me not to volunteer for anything so I did not even look at him. He said "Hey you, you are about to learn how to peel potatoes". I noticed he was looking at me so I followed him to the store room. He told me where to sit and I could rest my back on a machine that was there covered with a burlap sack. He showed me where there were nine one hundred pound bags of potatoes and he handed me a small peeler knife and as he started to leave said "have fun".

I labored all day on the nine hundred pounds of potatoes till my hands felt like the were webbed like duck feet. They were all pale and slimy. The Mess Steward came by and told me I had done a good job but he needed one more bag peeled. I figured enough was enough and told him I simply could not do any more. Instead of yelling at me like the previous want to be generals at the YMCA and reception station he said "O.K. take the burlap bag of the machine you have been leaning on all day and pour the last bag of potatoes into it and turn the button on."

When I turned the button on and all the potatoes came out nice and peeled and into a basket. Within a few minutes it was over. The bag was completely peeled and they looked beautiful. I said "Why could I not do it to the other nine bags"? "Because you said you did not know how to peel potatoes, now you do"! This had been one of those tough lessons that I had to learn, and I had. Where was the guy from GM that told me not to volunteer for any detail?

CHAPTER 9

Officer Candidate School

Well, I received my orders to attend OCS and I was still not sure what I was going to do there. I was to attend Infantry OCS at Ft. Benning, Georgia. When I arrived at Ft. Benning I was two weeks early for my class so I had to go to a Basic Training Company to help out training recruits for those two weeks. Meanwhile I worked on my uniforms and footwear. I shined my leather so well I could see myself on my boots and low quarters (shoes).

On my reporting date for OCS I took a taxi cab and arrived at the 64th OC Company. I barely opened the door to get out when there was a tall lieutenant in my face yelling all kind of bad words. Another want to be general, I thought. What is with this guys that yell all the time.

This was Lt. Noriega a six foot plus Hawaiian and he was going to make me feel welcomed. He kept on yelling at me as I unloaded my gear, frequently dropping me to do push ups. He kept on yelling at me as I made my way into the building to sign in. Inside there were other candidates being yelled at by other officers that were referred to as TACs. This was our welcoming reception. I guess there won't be any snacks and goodies today.

As more candidates arrived the special attention we were receiving got more watered down as the TACs had more victims to yell at and order around the building having them do push ups. It was a hectic day and one to remember for a lifetime. There were candidates running, crawling, and doing push-ups every where. And there was the chin-up bar outside the mess-hall.

I am standing outside the barracks of the 64th OC company at OCS.

At meal time it was a carnival around the chin-up bar as the TACs would be ganging up on the other Candidates yelling and giving orders. There was a Captain that stayed in the background that first day and that was the Company Commander of the 64th Officer Candidate Company, Capt. Ira D. Horton. He gave the impression of being a big condor sitting on a cliff ledge just waiting for a prey to be snatched up. In this case we were the prey. He was definitely the man in charge although right now he was letting the TACs handle the harassment.

The XO or Senior TAC was Lt. Jack W. Sorenson. He was a pretty big man way over six feet and meaner than a rattler. He was directing the first day blues for us. Once he had you under his grasp it was sad. At meal times he directed the activities against the candidates, The other eight TACs with the exception of Noriega were pretty good officers with a job to do and they were going to do it. The other officers were Lee F. Ciulla, Gary D. Bennett, Michael V. Lloyd, Marlin Coffee, Robert L. Sorem, Peter Russell and Lt. Sargent. As the course progressed we lost some officers to flight school and that was the reason we had extra TACs. My TAC in the sixth platoon Lt. Robert L. Sorem would leave for flight school and he was replaced by my old friend Paul Noriega. Our friendship never improved even thought we had gotten an early start the first day. Under Lt. Sorem things were great in the platoon, because he was an outstanding leader and a great human being. Lt. Sorem was a good example of an officer and a gentleman.

Besides our company TACs bringing smoke upon us, there were the third lieutenants or senior candidates or blue helmets. These were candidates that were in their last six weeks of training and they wore blue colored helmets to distinguish them from us. They had the authority to harass us anywhere they saw us. They could yell at us, make us do push-ups etc and there were many of them around the area.

The training at Infantry OCS was hard. There was intensified physical training and drill and ceremonies. Here time was irrelevant, if it had to be done it was done. The days were long and the nights were short and at the beginning there was no time off on week ends. And there was the running everywhere we went. Run, Run, Run. And then there was the low-crawling especially across from the barracks at a field where they trained the point dogs. There were dog feces everywhere, and we crawled thru them and they did not smell nice.

The training started with a bang with the academics being taught at Infantry Hall. We would be running in formation from the barracks to the hall. There, we arrived all sweated up and ready for class. As soon as class started you could see the heads swaying as the candidates were beginning to fall asleep. There were ten minute breaks every hour and it was run to the bathroom and then grab a quick coffee cup to stay awake during the next hour. At lunch time we would run back to the mess-hall, stand in line, get yelled at as we did our push-ups and chin-ups. Then it was double time back to Infantry Hall. Wow! By now our underarms were like a bowl of guacamole.

Right off the bat some candidates stood out over the rest of us. Usually they were the ones who had been prior service. There was a sharp staff sergeant named Cesta Ayers and a sergeant first class named James Williams, who would march and call cadence from the first day. These gentleman were sharp, but unfortunately they got the rash of yelling from the TACs. These men took a lot of attention away from us.

Officer Candidate Ayers was so sharp he was scary and the TACs were on his case constantly. SFC Williams had been a Green Beret with the commander Capt. Horton and there was no love between them, but Williams was on the receiving end of the commander's wrath.

I feel that many of us graduated from OCS because the attention was more directed at the prior service men than to us, not that we were not on the receiving end ourselves. These TACs seemed to be energized when one of us crossed their paths. When we ate, it was sitting on the front four inches of the chair and staring straight ahead without looking at our plates, meanwhile our friends the TACs were cruising between the tables yelling at us.

Capt. Horton and Lt. Sorenson would be sitting at the head table starring at us and giving us their evil look. They reminded me of hyenas watching their young eating a victim. One day Lt. Noriega, my old friend stopped in from of me and yelled "What are you starring at smack". "Nothing sir" I replied. "You are starring at me mud-face" he continued. "No Sir, I am not" I continued. "This will teach you to stare at me". He got a glass and poured it about half full with Tabasco Sauce. "Now drink it, you maggot" he said. I picked it up, drank the entire content, put down the glass and asked "May I have some more hot sauce Sir". He left mumbling something I would not repeat in church.

My roommate was a young man from St. Louis named Tom Vogel and a real nice friend he turned out to be. He had a musical pop band called the "Apollos" and he missed his music very much. On occasion he would get some candidates together and play for us. Tom knew the music business and was a good entertainer.

As the weeks went by we started to combine tactics with academics and weapons with drill and ceremonies. There was never a dull moment as the class schedules were mixed with trips to the ranges where we fired our M-14, the new M-16, the .45 pistol, the M-60 machinegun, the rifle grenade and the new M-79 grenade launcher, the .50 caliber machine gun and the .90MM recoilless rifle.

It was hectic and we still had the marching in formation and the physical training. We continued the physical combat training with hand to hand fighting and pugil sticks fighting as well as the long distance running and the obstacle course. .There was still the low crawl to contend with as well as the obstacle course, the monkey bars and the Leadership Reaction Course.

Meanwhile the academics were going at a faster pace and so were the tactics. We began to do samples of war scenarios with recent Viet-Nam returning Officers monitoring our progress. One day we were in Infantry Hall and we had a combined arms battle scenario. The instructor was a two time Viet-Nam Infantry Commander named Capt James Graham. The man was a heavily decorated veteran and it was obvious he new his stuff.

Capt Graham explained that in this scenario there was a company of infantry in heavy contact with the enemy. The troops were tired, hungry and were unable to move forward. There were many wounded that needed to be evacuated and the ammo was running low. He said he wanted someone to give him the solution to the problem. As I listen, I started to doze off and was not sure what I was hearing, but I was sitting almost to the rear of the large classroom.

All of a sudden I was falling asleep and put my head on my desk, then, I heard from far away "Will Officer Candidate Villarreal please come to the front and explain to the rest of the class what he would do in this case." I jerked up and realized everyone was looking toward me way in the back of the classroom. I started to walk toward the podium completely bewildered. I could see Capt. Graham trying to give me the pointer to show on the map what I would do. As I passed the student leader OC Ayers, he gave me a look of encouragement.

I got the pointer from Capt. Graham and he backed off and left me all alone in front of the map. "Sir, I will request B-52 strikes on the enemy. But first I will withdraw my troops to the east as it is the only route that is not blocked by the enemy. I will pull back three kilometers which is the safe distance for the B-52, then I will re-supply my men, feed them a hot meal and rest. After the strikes have passed and my troops are rested I will return to the battle area accompanied by gun ships and exploit the battle scene capturing or killing whatever is left from the enemy unit".

When I finished there was complete silence. I wondered if I had goofed and would be packing my bags that night. The only indication was the smile and proud look that OC Ayers was giving me. The entire class erupted in applause. Capt. Graham stepped up and took the pointer from me. "Well done" he said and I knew that at least for now I was staying in OCS. Little did I know that Capt Graham and I would live that exact scenario later in Viet-Nam.

Everything was not rosy, one day I failed the mortars FDC exam. Even thought I had failed it by one point I was recommended for removal from OCS. I would go before a panel of Commissioned Officers and they would recommend what was to be done with me. We were five students that were "Boarded" that day and the panel convened to decide our fate. When the Officers returned I was the only one retained as the other four candidates were dismissed and sent back to their units.

At that time we had taken part in a Tiger Tactics contest with the other OC companies. Whichever company was graded the most aggressive in our Tactical Operations would be awarded the title of "Tiger Tactics" and as a prize would appear in a movie John Wayne was filming at Ft. Benning as extras. Well the day of my panel was the day they announced the winner, and we came in second. Well so much for the Green Beret movie and John Wayne.

When I went to my bay and met with Tom Vogel we decided to go to Columbus and celebrate. Forget my panel and forget John Wayne, let's go have a big steak and the best restaurant for steaks was the Black Angus. We took a cab to the Black Angus and were received by special security that told us the Angus was close while John Wayne was filming because he ate all his meals there. Well, if that did not add an insult to injury. So we went to a sand witch sing along bar there in Columbus. Soon we would be receiving our blue helmets and forget about all this.

One evening I heard a lot of yelling in the stairwell and it was Lt. Sorenson yelling at Cesta Ayers for something or other. A few days later the TACs apprehended a wife placing candy and goodies in a bucket so that her husband OC Joe Williams could pull it up to his room with a rope. He assumed the nickname of "Poagy Bait" that evening and she was ridiculed by the Officers as if she was a Candidate herself and the contraband well it was eaten by the TACs.

The stress was terrible as we got deeper into the Infantry subjects and candidates were resigning right and left. One Candidate committed suicide one evening to ad to our woes. We continued to run but the runs were longer and more painful as most of the time our rucksacks were full of rocks. The low-crawling at Raiders Creek was terrible as the sand would cling to our wet uniforms. The TACs would run us down some rural roads while they rode in a jeep yelling at us. Occasionally one or two of them would show their fiber and run with us, without the rucksack full of rocks.

We finally received Senior Candidate status and our blue helmets. Now we could walk like normal people even in uniform. The TACs slowed down their harassment and treatment was overall better. We were allowed more free time and more slack at bed checks. We even wandered off to see an Auburn University football game. Graduation was nearing and we were measured for our officer uniforms which were expensive especially the dress blues.

There was still plenty of training and it was getting more intensified. One day the CO Capt. Horton blew a fuse or something because we asked for more toilet paper. He read us the Army Regulation pertaining to that and were reminded but we were to be issued one square of toilet paper per day unless we were females. So with that in mind we purchased our own toilet paper for the duration of the course.

Well the big day arrived and we dressed up for graduation. It was November, 5, 1967 and I had been in the Army an eternity or so it seemed, in reality it was under fourteen months. We all looked so different in our new fitted uniforms and our saucer caps with the gold trim. Wow! We were Second Lieutenants in the U.S. Army, were leaders of men, well not so fast Vic, you still have to prove yourself.

With graduation came our new assignments. Tom Vogel would go to Baltimore and training at the Intelligence School. I would go to Fort Bliss and be a Basic Training Officer. Another Officer Lt. Kenny Dies would also go with me but to a different training Brigade. We went on leave and would report to Ft. Bliss later. So off to Laredo, Texas for a couple of weeks. I took a bus from Nuevo Laredo to Sabinas to see my parents. Ironically on the bus were the two ROTC Instructors from Martin High, Capt Roberto Flores and Lt. Armando Garcia and their wives. They were on a short vacation to Monterrey, Mexico. I had always admired these men and when they were in uniform I was all envy and wished that I had enrolled in ROTC.

CHAPTER 10

Duty at Fort Bliss, Texas

In late November I reported to Ft. Bliss, Texas. Kenny Dies and I met at a motel off IH-10 and spent the night there before reporting in to the post. Kenny was interested in finding a six-pack of Coors Beer since it was not sold in Beaumont. That done we joked and wondered what awaited us the next day. Kenny wanted to go to flight school and did not plan on being at Bliss very long.

We reported in at the Post Headquarters and Kenny was assigned to the Training Brigade on the main post and I was assigned to the one at Logan Heights. We were assigned as roommates at the Bachelor Officer Quarters. We were assigned a two bedroom apartment with complete kitchen and living room and bathroom. The quarters were actually very nice.

I reported to the Training Brigade and met the commander Col. Richardson, who was being replaced by Col. Zanin. He sent me down to the 1st Battalion and I met LTC Eli Veazy who was the Battalion Commander. He decided to assign me to A Company as a training officer. There was an officer there already named Bill Williams and the company commander was 1Lt Duane Emmert. Emmert was a returnee from Korea and a very pleasant fellow.

I started my duties as the outside training officer while Williams was the inside officer and took care of all the training schedules and records. I would handle all the physical training, drill and ceremonies and rifle ranges. This was fine with me as I wanted to prove what a great shape I was in. Every morning by five o'clock I was there the first to turn on the lights and watch as the recruits run around half asleep getting ready for physical training. Then they were falling outside to get into formation. It was dark and cold but nice to be there. The yelling by the Drill Sergeants was intimidating and, boy, did I remember that part of my training.

The weeks went by and the recruits started to take shape. Pretty soon they were marching very well and could sing cadence also. Their shooting skills were coming along as were their academic classes. I had to teach Military Justice and the Code of Conduct. The trainees were also getting ready for the Proficiency Test as well as their physical test. I also met a good number of their parents who went to visit them during the weekends.

Christmas was upon us but I had reported recently so I had to stay. The recruits were going home for a few days so I was the Duty Officer responsible for seeing them off. One group of busses had only gone a couple of hours when one overturned near Sierra Blanca and several recruits were killed. I was sent on a jeep to go to the scene and I nearly froze on the way over there. When I got there the DPS were investigating the accident and I was given a quick report by a patrolman named Dale Squint on the accident and the injured and dead.(I was to meet this officer again many years later while in the U.S. Border Patrol).

The battalion officers were very united since LTC Veazy ran a pretty tight ship, but just like we trained hard we partied hard. Many parties were thrown by the company commanders as well as the battalion commander and we as young officers enjoyed them all. In Company D there was an officer by the name of Eliseo Baeza who was a local man from El Paso and he was a party all by himself. He was very jolly and funny. He made our parties a lot of fun and even introduced the rest of us to some local foods enjoyed in that area. Eliseo was a very enthusiastic eater and he made sure we had plenty to eat at the parties.

Taking the recruits to the many ranges at Ft. Bliss was a chore since they were so far away in the desert. The firing in the winter was somewhat hard since the winds would come up and they were pretty chilly. One day I took the recruits for a trek in the desert and when I returned I found my car still in the parking lot but it was grey instead of light blue. The sand storm that came up had changed the color of my car. Thank you, USAA for painting my car back to the original color.

Finally we graduated the first group of recruits. They were very happy and ready to attend their advance training. Some were a bit apprehensive about the Viet-Nam War and wondered if they would be going. There were numerous American Indians in our groups of training perhaps because Ft. Bliss was so close to the reservations. Many of the Indians had Spanish surnames especially the Pueblos and Navajos. Many of these recruits had not finished high school and I enrolled them in GED classes and while I was at Ft. Bliss, 82 of them received their completion certificate.

There were more groups of recruits coming in. I would accompany the Drill Sergeants to the reception station to pick our groups. Then the cycle would start all over again with the yelling, running, marching etc. In the groups were some recruits that were of special interest. One day one of the Jose Greco Dancers was in the cycle and he did not hesitate to entertain the rest of the trainees. Occasionally we would get some one that had been a musician or singer and again they would entertain the rest.

I found the people of El Paso as a general rule very friendly and they would not hesitate to invite you to their home for dinner or other festivities. One day in trying to solve the problem that a recruit had I met a family name Veliz. Before long I was invited to eat at their home and the friendship went on for several months. The father was a musician who often played at outings and I enjoyed their family company very mush.

After three cycles of recruits that we processed through A Company, LTC Veazy called me in an told me that the commander from C Company was leaving and he wanted me to replace him. Of the twenty companies in the Brigade only one was commanded by a 1LT all the rest were Captains, so for a 2nd Lt. to take over a company was a good shot in the arm for me. I accepted and moved over to C Company and to begin competing against my old friends Williams and Emmert at A Company.

Meanwhile my dear friend Kenny Dies had left for flight school. I remained alone in the government apartment and was never assigned a new roommate. Never in my wildest dreams did I think I would see

Kenny again especially in the way we would meet again. Well I started my new assignment with a bang when my top NCO was found to be an alcoholic. I thought nothing could beat that except my company clerk forged my name on some orders for 30 days vacation. Just when I needed them more I lost them and the annual inspection was just around the corner. Well, we made it thru all that and my company was declared the Honor Company, having edged out my old A Company. LTC Veazy had a smile from ear to ear.

Apparently LTC Veazy had taken some criticism for appointing me to a company when the other companies for the most part were commanded by Captains except for A Company. I was glad I had come though for the Old Man.

I had also made a personal contribution to the training brigade. In the previous cycles of trainees I had notice a high rate of failures on the Proficiency Test. After close observation I notice the failures came from the trainees being nervous at the time of the test. I asked LTC Veazy if I could experiment with the testing and he gave his approval.

In the experiment I asked the different companies for two drill instructors each to formulate a test cadre. These men would test the trainees the day before the actual test therefore if a trainee was nervous and made a mistake it was on a practice test and not the real one. My company was the first to go through the experiment and on the day of the test we had zero failures.

The experiment was made available to the other companies and the results were surprisingly good. The Battalion Commander was all smiles with the results. While the testing was going on I received orders for Viet-Nam.

I started to get my shots and teeth fixed. I had never been to a dentist so it was a complicated matter. The nurse was trying to place an ex-ray film when I accidentally bit her. She left the room crying and soon a huge fat major came out and said he was the dentist and that if I bit the nurse again he would punch me in the mouth. I figured this guy must have worked at the YMCA also. He instructed the nurse to shoot me up again with Novocain.

When I left the dental clinic I could not feel that I had a mouth or face for that matter as I was so numbed by the injections. I knew I had to get back to the rifle ranges to finish the day so I ducked into a PX snack bar. I ordered a bowl of Chile and started to eat when I noticed a tall NCO kept staring at me.

Finally he approached my table and said. "Do you feel OK Lieutenant"?, "Yes I feel fine", I lied. "Well the reason I asked is because you have Chile running out of your mouth and down your fatigue shirt" he replied. I was so embarrassed and looked at him as he looked very familiar and asked "Are you by chance from Laredo, Texas and do you have two brothers that are teachers there"? He answered "Yes, I'm Francisco Ibarra and my brothers Roberto and Rodolfo are teachers one at L.J. Christen and the other at Martin High school". How embarrassing I thought, this man is related to my teachers and now he sees me with Chile running out of my mouth and down the front of my shirt. A fourth brother Juan Ibarra (El Teco) was my high school classmate and was also serving in the Army.

Before leaving for Viet-Nam, I was to attend Jungle Expert School in Panama and then proceed to the Republic of South Viet-Nam. I was not surprised because most young officers were being sent over to jungle school and then to Viet-Nam. My main concern was how to tell my parents. I decided to tell them I was going to Panama and instructed my brothers and sisters not to tell them the truth. I knew my mother was not in the best of health and to have her worrying about me being in Viet-Nam might be too much on her. I flew to California to say goodbye to Ofelia and Carlos, and their two girls Nora and Nelda.

After a very nice party by the Battalion Officers I said my goodbyes. LTC Veazy made a nice speech and I said goodbye to Eliseo and the other officers of the other companies. I took some time off to go to Laredo and Sabinas. Somehow I managed to keep Mom and Dad from knowing the truth. Linda and her parents knew the truth but I instructed them not to let it out to my parents. I knew my mother well and if she suspected that I was in the war zone it could affect her health.

Chapter 11

Jungle School in Panama

After using all of my leave I reported in for the trip to Panama. After an all day of waiting and then boarding the plane for the trip we arrived in Panama City at night. When we arrived there had been a small revolution and there were still rebels out in the jungle. Of course we had to travel to Colon on the eastern side of the country when Panama City is on the western. We were placed on a toy like train to cross the country. The train was so small we barely fit one person and our equipment per row.

We arrived in Colon and were quickly picked up by military trucks for the trip to Fort Sherman. There were military roadblocks along the road to keep the rebels out. This thing was serious here. We were taken to these huge cement barracks by the coast. The bay waters were right outside the barracks. All things considered this was a beautiful place. There were several large structures with two floors for sleeping and one had the mess hall and club.

We started the two week course with a bang. First there was the training on how to survive in the jungle. Then there was what you could eat in the jungle like fruits and animals. We actually had to sample the animals and snakes and fruits and vegetables. To me this was the best part of the course since I had eaten most of the animals and fruits while living in Mexico and in the ranches where Father worked near Big Wells. I was fascinated with some new comers to the menu like menke which were big rabbit like rats and monkeys. Eating papayas, mangos and bananas was pure pleasure. Others like cacti and tunas (cactus pear) I had eaten for years and still do.

We went on a hike in the jungle and soon I found a lemon tree whose lemons were larger than grapefruits. I ate some and carried some off for later. One of the NCOs kept looking at me eating the lemons and asked me for one. Later, I took some ripe bananas off a tree and ate them and he kept on looking at me. Finally he asked me where I got them from and I pointed to a banana tree. He got his machete and chop off a huge banana bunch.

We moved out and he continued to carry the bunch with him, we crossed a couple of streams and there he went carrying his heavy load. Meanwhile I got some more ripe bananas and he tried to eat the ones he had. Finally several days later he asked me when his bananas would ripen, and I said "In a couple of months". He looked confused and asked me why mine ripen so fast. I quickly responded that I was picking the ripe ones and at each occasion and I would select from a new tree only the ones that were ripe. He felt like a fool and really he looked like one carrying the bunch of green bananas.

We did some other training that was mostly fun. One night we went on bivwack into the jungle to get used to the outdoors. We had to set up our hammocks about two feet off the ground to keep the snakes and other varmints from crawling into our beds. Late that night a screaming gorilla that was in one of the trees that we tied the hammocks to fell asleep in the tree and fell off on top of one sleeping NCO. Well you can imagine the surprise to both as they both took off screaming in different directions.

Another event that was mostly fun was the boa constrictor handling. We were taken to the Fort Stewart Zoo, placed in the bleachers and then a big Green Beret instructor appeared. Two other Berets came out and very ceremoniously closed the main gate to a six-foot fence. When the demonstrator appeared he had a big boa wrapped around him. The instructor said that before graduation from Jungle School we would all have to handle the snake in the same manner. At that time two NCOs jumped from the bleachers and scaled the six-foot fence and ran all the way to the barracks. Actually all you had to do was press behind the head of the snake and it would release you. Those two guys did not wait around to find out.

We proceeded with our training which consisted with repelling down a small waterfall that was very slippery and we got all wet doing it. Then there was the slide for life where we traveled on a pulley very fast across the Chagres River. We departed from a very tall mahogany tree and traveled at a high speed, we kept straightening our flight by shifting our bodies until we crossed the river. At the other end was waiting a big knot on the rope that stopped us on a dime and then we dropped into the river and swam to shore.

The final big event was to build a raft out of some brush and a poncho liner and swim back across the Chagres. There was a new factor in the event, you could see the fins of some sharks waiting for us downriver. There were two small boats with riflemen to protect us. We were not told that there was an electronic fence that was not visible to us keeping the sharks away from us. When I jumped in I could see the sharks moving around in a frenzy. Even though I could not swim I pushed the raft in front of me so fast that I came out first on the other side. I did not know whether sharks like Mexican food (me), but I did not want to find out.

That weekend we had time off but with the revolution going on no one was allowed to go into Colon. Well one of the Green Berets a Lt. Lopez and I had become good friends He invited me to go into town and told me to tell the guards that I worked in the kitchen in Spanish. Everything worked well and I sneaked into Colon. I was able to purchase some souvenirs to bring back. There was sign all over town of the revolution they had just had. Store fronts had broken glass and there were bullet marks all over the walls. A theater had been sprayed with gun fire, ironically the movie was, *The Green Berets* with John Wayne.

Now we were ready to face the second week which was mostly the Escape and Evasion Course. In the course we were expected to move thru jungle and mountainous terrain that was occupied by the enemy. We would be armed with a compass and a machete and our good judgment. We were to practice every thing we had learned the 1st week and during our lives. The enemy would be a group of Green Berets that would go to some extremes to get us to give up information, but only if they caught us. We were given coordinates to where some food was hidden and it was up to us to find it.

An Army truck dropped us off on a gravel road without even stopping. We went in groups of three into the jungle and further up the road they dropped more groups. We dashed into the jungle and went some hundred meters and stopped to regroup and plan our strategies. I would be the group leader and direct our way into the jungle. The other two would take turns chopping the jungle where we could not walk thru. They were to listen for any strange sounds or voices that might indicate that the captors were nearby.

I directed the group to the first cache of buried food and the direction to the next plot. We eat and proceeded on course. We got near a small river but I new that it was infested with crocodiles so I looked for an easier way to cross. I found a large mahogany tree that had fallen over the entire river and decided it was the best place to cross. I decided to wait a while and rest in the thick jungle near the tree.

About that time we heard voices and the sounds of the jungle being chopped away. We did not have long to wait as another team neared the tree and started to cross on it. When they got to the other side they were received by a group on captors that physically assaulted them and took them prisoners. We were so close that we heard the captors saying that they were taking them to the prisoner compound and then returning again for some others that might cross there.

As soon as the voices died down we quickly ran across the tree and were safe on the other side. We proceeded into the jungle and soon came up a big hill that we had to crawl up to get to the top. I was in the lead and grabbed a small tree that disintegrated with my pulling on it. I heard the other two men yelling as the tree was full of ants that landed on them. We came up a small creek with clear water and here we cleaned ourselves of the ants and had a refreshing break.

Now it was night time and we were having problems moving thru the jungle, because besides the thick vegetation, jungle creatures, there were sharp drops in the terrain. The worst enemy was a tree called black palm, which was a palm tree covered with black needles that were very sharp and when you collided with it the needles would break of on your flesh and numb your arms and legs.

During the night we found some groups resting for the night and we joined them since numbers meant strength. One of the men was a straggler from a group that had been captured but he had gotten away in the darkness. In escaping he had run smack into a black palm tree and was badly hurt. We could not leave him behind so we took him with us and now we were about thirteen and we figured we could outwrestle the Green Berets.

We traveled all day finding the food plots and continuing knowing that if we could find the food the enemy must know where it was hidden. We would rest only when necessary and continue our trek. We would occasionally hear yelling as other groups were caught some times we were so close we could hear the captors talking and laughing of what they were going to do to them.

Our sick member was getting worse as those stickers from the black palm were getting infected. We decided to hole up in some thick jungle for the second night and avoid getting more persons hurt. Water was not a problem as there were creeks with running water everywhere and like a clock it would rain at midnight.

The third day we started to move very early as we figured that the captors were drinking that army coffee and would start in the late morning. Besides they had to interrogate all the prisoners. As we went for maybe two hours we came up on a wide gravel road like the one they had dropped us at the start of the course. I realized we had completed the course with out getting caught. We came out of the jungle and a military truck picked us up and took us to Fort Sherman. We were some of the first to finish, and we were able to get medical attention for our injured member.

When we got to Sherman we cleaned up and went to the club to celebrate. It would be more that a day wait for all the groups to come in, if they did not get lost. At the club were some men that had been captured and tortured and finally released. They told their horrible stories of their capture. Apparently the Green Berets were running the camp like a real prisoner of war camp.

Upon capture they would ask you some questions and if you did not cooperate they would have a man smack you until you either talked or they passed you to the next station. At next station they would blind fold you and throw you into a mud pit full of boas. The boas had their heads cut off but since you were blind folded you could not tell. The pit was also full of mud with the snakes moving around and squeezing the men.

The last station for those that had not talked was where the captors would drop a drop of acid onto your manhood. As far as I was told everyone captured with the exception of a Native American talked while in captivity. We were lucky that we had not been captured. It had been a tough training exercise. We started to pack our bags for the return trip to the United States.

We would have a few days off before going on to San Francisco and departing for Viet-Nam.

Chapter 12

Arrival In Viet-Nam

In early November of 1968 I arrived in South Viet-Nam but we were received by a rocket attack and had to run from the plane to the shelters. After the rockets subsided we were able to grab our bags and run to a military bus waiting for us to take us to Ben Hoa. Somehow riding in a bus toward Ben Hoa unharmed was not the greatest feeling for me. Finally, we arrived and went to some tents to wait there as we were issued jungle fatigues and boots. We went about getting name tags etc.

We were placed in an Army theater while we waited our assignments. A classmate from OCS Jon Hendrickson and I were sitting together waiting for our assignment. We chatted about the year we had spent stateside as young officers. Soon the assignments started to come in. We looked at each other and said "as long as we don't go to the 1st Air Cavalry", we would be happy. They called out the assignments for the 1st Infantry, 173rd Airborne, the 101st Airborne, the 198th and 199th Light Infantry Brigades, the 25 Infantry, the 82nd Airborne, and the 9th Infantry. Now Jon and I were the only ones left in the Theater when the assignment NCO came in and said "Hendrickson and Villarreal to the 1st Cavalry Division". Right away we knew we were going to the most go getter Division in Viet-Nam.

We were flown to An Khe the Cavalry Division Headquarters and training facility. There we were for a few days going on patrols and mainly getting familiar with our issued weapons. It was not long we were flown to Quan Loi and our assignment with the 12th Cavalry. We were picked up at the airstrip in a jeep by an NCO that I now believe was Lonnie Murdock. He took us to the 2 Bn 12thCav Headquarters to meet the commander and get our individual assignments.

Lt. Jon Hendrickson was assigned to B Co (Bad Bet) and quickly departed for his unit. Before I went in a Lt. Murgia went in to talk to the Commander and after a short conversation came out and addressed me. The young officer was gripping to the CO that he was an armor officer assigned to an infantry unit and would not be awarded a CIB (Combat Infantry Badge). The CO was not impressed with Murgia's point of argument.

I was asked to enter the Commander's tent: he was located toward the rear of the command tent. It appeared to me that the commander was about forty years and in the prime of his life. "Lt. Villarreal is that name Spanish"? he asked. "Yes it is, but I am a Mexican", I replied. LTC James Dingeman was the Battalion Commander for my new assignment the 2nd of the 12th Cavalry. He assigned me to C Company (Wild Card) and asked me if I had any questions (LTC Dingeman gave me the impression that he was hell on wheels as a commander). I replied that I did not and off I went to my unit since it was getting dark and they were guarding the water point outside Quan Loi.

In a jeep I was taken to meet my Company Commander, NCOs and the soldiers. The Company Commander was Capt. John Emrath. He was about thirty years of age. The 1st platoon leader was 1Lt. Peter Tripp a blond fellow. The other officers were Lt. Murgia from Los Angeles and of Mexican descent who was platoon leader for the second platoon and Lt. Schlifta, who was platoon leader for the third platoon. Capt Emrath told me I would replace Lt. Tripp on the 1st platoon and Tripp would be the XO.

After meeting the Officers I went to the line to meet my platoon. The platoon sergeant was SFC Alberto Rodriguez. The machine gun NCO was SSG Conrado Avila. The 1st squad leader was SGT Dan Griffin a tall slim NCO. The 2nd squad leader was SGT John Perkins a quite but effective NCO. Rodriguez was from Colorado while Griffin was from New York. Avila and Perkins were from Texas.

I also met some of the men as others were on listening posts. I met my radio Operator, Harold Hopper from Alabama. Hopper was a true country boy and a very sincere person, I could not have done better if I had selected him myself. I also met George (Joe) Rubadeau and John Nurse, Parrish, Duane Hipple and Johnny Heath. Heath would turned out to be quite a character. Then there was Rubadeau who walked with a youthful bounce as if he had new shock observers, and Parrish would alternate as point man every other day and referred to everyone as "Hoss". Both of these men were surefooted and eagle eyed.

There was also a man named Brewer, and Walter Hoxworth a M-60 gunner and the list went on and on (unfortunately my memory fades at times.)

Johnny Heath was a M-60 gunner who was either high on booze or high on some other substance, but put in a tight spot if you pointed him in the right direction he could smoke the enemy with the machine gun, and there was no shortage of guts when facing the enemy.

I settled down for the evening as SFC Rodriguez and I talked about the strengths and weakness of the men assigned to the 1st Platoon. There was no attempt on the water point that evening and in the morning we were replaced by another platoon from our company and we ventured out on a search and destroy operation not far from Quan Loi. We actually traveled around the camp to the other side and there we entered the Michelin Rubber Plantation. The Michelin was a rubber plantation that covered thousands of square miles of rubber trees.

The first night in the Michelin, Capt Emrath sent us on ambush. He left it up to me where to have it and I picked a large trail coming into the plantation and in direction of Quan Loi. I figured that if the enemy came to get closer to Quan Loi they would come from that direction. I saw many tracks of Ho Chi Ming slicks (slicks were primitive shoes made of tire rubber and leather throngs, they were called *huaraches* in Spanish) so we placed claymore mines making some kill zones in front of us.

We were a few hundred meters from the main perimeter and hiding behind the rubber trees and the shadows created by the giant trees. About midnight I saw an enemy soldier sneak out from the jungle and toward our kill zone. He was the enemy point man and soon made a hand signal for the others to follow. A steady line of North Vietnamese soldiers in kaki uniforms followed carrying rockets toward Quan Loi.

All of a sudden a very tall soldier stepped out of the jungle and headed for the front of the enemy column. He was some kind of officer by his actions and his uniform appeared to be different that the others.

The tall enemy soldier traveled to the front of the column and started to bark orders and then he pointed toward our hidden location. I knew he could not see us because it was very dark under the rubber trees. I could almost see his face because he was near the road and the moonlight was hitting him on the face. He kept on moving and pointing in our direction when I realized he was right in front of one of our claymore mines. I was very excited and with a lump in my throat I squeezed the claymore switch.

There was a very loud explosion and the enemy soldier was swept away and then my men opened up and started to mow the enemy soldiers down while they were in the kill zone. Soon the only ones left were the ones retreating back to the jungle in high speed. As soon as it started the firefight was over, it did not last a minute in duration. We approached the fallen soldiers to exploit the scene. I was all excited and found my self yelling in victory, "Viva the United States, Viva Laredo, Viva Mexico".

All of sudden Hopper gave me the microphone and said it was the Commander. He said "1-6 what in world is going on". I responded that we had sprung the ambush on a platoon size unit and we had killed several enemy soldiers without having any casualties. "So you are having a celebration or what, I hear all the yelling" he added. I realized I was very excited and had already started to celebrate with out considering a counter attack by the enemy.

I looked down at my trophy, who was not very big now as the claymores had taken both legs off. He had red artillery insignia on his shoulder boards and I realized he was the rocket man. He was also a black Chinese soldier because the men told me he was a Manchurian judging by his size. I reached over and took his belt buckle off with the star inscribed on it (which I would wear on my uniform until the end of my tour.)

We collected the weapons of the dead enemy soldiers (7) and retreated to our main perimeter and the waiting arms of Capt Emrath. He quickly debriefed me and made his report to LTC Dingeman who could hear the explosions from Quan Loi. As I went to settle down

Capt Emrath said "Good job 1-6, but next time no celebration". I realized that killing enemy soldiers was just a job for the Captain, but how could I explain how excited I had been, after all I had never killed anyone. I guess I was no longer an FNG. I also guessed that every one must feel that excitement in their first encounter with the enemy and their first kill.

The days around Quan Loi continued with sporadic skirmishes with the enemy. Once we marched thru a small village and the villagers were all smiling and waving their hands at us and that made us feel good. When we went past the village and into the jungle Capt. Emrath received instructions to go back the same way and make camp on the other side of the village. I was bringing up the rear of the Company and now I was in the lead. As we reentered the village the villagers were already hugging and celebrating with an enemy unit. The shooting started and we had to go hut by hut to clear the village and we realized those people were not our friends but enemy sympathizers.

CHAPTER 13

The Johnny Heath Circus

That evening we set up camp near the village and I sent one of the squads and an M-60 machine gun on ambush on a main trail leading to the village. About midnight SGT Dan Griffin called that the M-60 gunner Johnny Heath had movement in front and was going to engage. I told him to hold on and see what else happened. A few minutes later Griffin called again that Johnny had movement and he thought they were elephants carrying rockets toward Quan Loi. Not knowing if the sighting was true or a product of whatever Johnny had smoked earlier, I asked him to be patient. About that time I heard a long burst of the M-60 augmented by small arms fire and a few grenades from the M-79. Also there was the weirdest sound of elephants in agony coming from the ambush site.

Johnny Heath in one of his better moods.

Sgt. Dan Griffin as usual—ready for action.

Yes, in the morning there was a dead elephant with two 222 rockets straddled on him. There was sign and a blood trail where another beast had limped away with his load. The handlers had not put up a fight, maybe they were discouraged by the gunner's long blast on the machine gun. Johnny Heath was a hero the next morning and he told and retold the story as he stroked his mustache handlebars with one hand and patted his M-60 with the other. What a character I had inherited when I was assigned as platoon leader for the first platoon. A few nights later Johnny was on ambush and reported that he had heavy movement in front of him and he was ready to engage. I told SGT Griffin to keep him from firing, but again to no avail as he opened up because they were so close he could see them. The burst of the machinegun quieted everything and we rested the rest of the night. In the morning when they searched the area they counted one dead wild game rooster.

Christmas was nearing and the men were in a jolly mood even under the conditions we were facing. On a search and destroy mission we had to cross a big open field with a lot of briars full of stickers. As the point man advanced through the briar patch all of a sudden he opened up on fully automatic. I wanted to know what happened and he said he nailed a *gook* hiding in the briar patch.

As we approached, we located the *gook*. Well, it was really a dead doe. Everyone laughed at the point man and they wanted to eat the animal. We got to the opposite tree line and made camp. Johnny Heath offered to gut the animal and slow roast her over a pit full of coals. I refused his offer and put two men to prepare the animal for a slow roast overnight and we would eat it in the morning.

Johnny kept approaching the fire and offering his expertise. In the morning I noticed the two men cooking the animal were asleep and the animal was missing a ham. I suspected Johnny had taken a big Bowie knife he had and sliced a leg off and had eaten it during the night. My suspicions grew even more when it was time to get a piece of the deer, and Johnny was too tired and sleepy to participate in the feast. OH Boy! What a character. I guess we can safely close the chapter of the wild man Johnny Heath.

CHAPTER 14

What are you doing laying down there 1-6?

One evening as we got ready to settle down for the evening, I sent out my LPs and then Quan Loi came under rocket attack and some probes on the perimeter line. Capt Emrath was like a guard dog on a tight leach as he wanted to do a night move and engage the enemy. We could see the Huey gun ships come over us to engage the enemy. I called SFC Rodriguez and SSG Avila for a quick meeting. We were sitting under a large rubber tree and my medic also joined the conversation about possibly moving at night.

All of a sudden a Huey came over us as if to engage the enemy with rockets or machine gun fire. As we looked up a large explosion was heard as a rocket or mortar fell between the group. The medic was grabbing his knees and SSG Avila was laid out flat on the ground as if dead, with a serious head wound. I had been blown backward against a rubber tree and SFC Rodriguez was miraculously untouched. I felt my chest hot and sticky and I suspected a chest wound but I had no pain. I later found out that it was milky warm rubber from the rubber tree next to me and not blood.

SSG Conrado Avila, Killen, Texas machine gun
crew leader looking for his pants.

SSG John Perkins, Liberty ,Texas.

SSG Avila was seriously hurt and I had to get help for him. With the firefight in progress that was going to be difficult. I left SFC Rodriquez with the two wounded and went to look for the commander. I was crawling to avoid the incoming small arms fire as I looked for him. In the darkness and gun smoke lit only by an occasional candle flare from the passing gun ships, I spotted him. I started crawling toward him but I was going to be lucky not to get hit by the enemy's small arms fire which had bullets flying everywhere.

I had heard wild stories about this man, but now, I was watching him in action. I crawled next to him and told him I was going to have to take my wounded somewhere to get extracted by a med-a-vac. He looked down at me and said, "What are you doing laying down there1-6? Get up, this is where the action is." My impression of Capt. Emrath never changed after that, he was either a very brave man or a complete fruit. He told me, "Do what you have to, I'm staying here and finishing off these *gooks,* I love to kill *gooks* (enemy soldiers). I crawled back to my wounded and ordered my platoon to get ready to move out even though we were still under fire.

I had to see if I could save SSG Avila who by now had lost a lot of blood. I looked back and could still see Capt Emrath under poor visibility shouting orders to the men and insults to the enemy. This was the same man that had admonished me for yelling at my first firefight.

I took my platoon about one kilometer thru a gap in the enemy soldiers. I personally carried SSG Avila while SFC Rodriguez carried the medic. That left the men free to fight the enemy if it came to that. Somehow we got through to an open area to have the wounded airlifted in a chopper. We never saw them again as Avila was sent to the states for his head wounds. I would not see SSG Avila until some twenty years later.

We rotated to pull security back at Quan Loi and rest for about a week. For me, it was a chance to get to know the men better. I was assigned an artillery forward observer name Alvin Burt from Ft. Worth, Texas, and he and I would become close friends as he was a very likeable young man and well verse in the art of calling in artillery.

One day I found a bunch of soldiers near LTC Dingeman's tent with Lt. Murgia.

The young officer was frying some corn tortillas and making tacos for the men. Everyone was having a good time as Murgia fried the tortillas in a canteen cup and filled them with meat and cheese and passed them out to the men. After he closed his food line I asked him why he was doing it. Obviously, he had to buy the El Paso brand tortillas and the other ingredients. He said "I do it for two reasons, one, the men love to eat my tacos, and two, when the men bunch up around me, the Commander hates it.".

CHAPTER 15

The River Boats

We were given travel orders that we were going to go work the river boats on the Saigon River near Cu Chi. The Chinooks picked us up at Quan Loi for the trip south. We landed and quickly boarded the Navy gunboats. This was going to be our home for a while since no one knew for how long.

Life was different going up and down the river and expecting a B-40 or RPG (Rocket Propelled Grenade) at any moment. The Navy men on the boats had their routine as they would be spotting and doing recon by fire with the boat's weapons. The boats were armed with .50 caliber machine guns, flame throwers and M-60s. Some were armed with quad 50s machine guns. Occasionally, we would receive and incoming round, but what the Navy shot in return to the threat was scary. Ammo was not in short supply on the PT boats and the gunners would pour a return fire that was enough to frighten any size force.

After any alteration with the enemy I would dismount the men and do a through search of the area, looking for bodies or weapons. Most of the time who ever had fired at the boats was long gone. The area was saturated with electronic equipment that had been dropped from the air to monitor enemy movements.

One day as I was exploiting an area where the enemy was supposed to be, I ran into Lt. Jon Hendrickson checking the same area. Although our meeting was brief, he told me that he had been wounded and had recuperated somewhat from his injuries. He was not a happy camper, maybe he was still hurting from the injuries.

One morning the men were dragging their feet as we were about to dismount and clear an area. I placed my self on the bow of the boat and started to entertain them by doing John Wayne impersonations. I was really loaded down with my ammo and gear as I stood there and the boat approached the bank. I said to them, "Come on pilgrims, we are going to kick their fannies". I was doing a western drawl as I spoke. At the same time the boat hit the bank and bounced back and I lost my balance and fell into the river. Since I had a heavy load of gear, I quickly sank into the muddy waters. As the men laughed at my expense, they hurriedly fished me out of the river soaking wet. What had been meant as a short entertaining episode turned into a story to be told and retold by my men.

CHAPTER 16

Sabor a Mi (It tastes like Me)

We worked around Cu Chi for several weeks and things were different here as most of our encounters were with the Viet-Cong and not the North Vietnamese Army or NVA like in the Michelin. The skirmishes were of a hit and run by the enemy. We would get sniper fire and as we tried to engage, the enemy would disappear into the small hamlets that were all over as small groups of families cultivated the rice paddies. Trying to distinguish a Viet-Cong guerrilla from a rice farmer was very hard.

One day as we crossed a long and flooded rice paddy and we were the lead platoon my point man came upon some reeds dividing one paddy from the other. We were up to our waist in the flooding of the paddy and moving was very hard. The point man (George Rubadeau) looked thru the reeds and ran a cross the last stretch onto dry land of a nearing hamlet. The M-79 man backing him up looked and did the same. I was curious and next in line and as I peered thru the reeds I was confronted with a huge water buffalo that had been tied on the other side of the reeds and had now broken loose and was charging toward me.

Well I turned to run thinking that I was a Mexican but not a bull fighter and I collided with Harold Hopper who was loaded down with the radio and all his personal gear. I had actually knocked him into the slush of the rice paddy and for sure would be crushed by the on coming buffalo. I turned to face the animal and switched my Car-15 into full automatic and started firing letting the beast have all twenty eight rounds. It went down with a big splash but was still moving, but I was so mad I pulled out my 45 pistol and fired all six rounds into the animals' head. Well it was dead now so I turned to pick up Hopper when he handed me the radio mike and said it was the CO.

Capt Emrath was yelling into the mike "What the hell is going on 1-6". I responded by telling him I had just killed a water buffalo. "What the hell man, this is not a Safari", he responded. I looked back and I could see the Capt. with mud all over and could understand why he was upset. I got my men out of the rice paddy and everyone was account for. All of a sudden a villager approached me and started to point a finger at me and saying "You number 10 GI". He was apparently the village chief and wanted to know who was responsible for killing his beast. I pointed my pistol at him at which he began yelling what I imagined were Vietnamese bad words. I ignored him and he disappeared into the village, and I thought good riddance.

Within an hour after he left a Huey approached our location and landed. An American Advisor got out and went into the village only to return soon after accompanied by the Village Chief. The Village Chief pointed to me and the dead animal. The advisor who was a Capt. approached me.

"Did you kill this buffalo", he said.

"It was either him or me and I'm glad it was the buffalo", I answered.

"Do you have any idea what you did", he continued.

"Yes, I have a pretty good idea, I shot him twenty-eight times with my AR and six rounds from my pistol", I answered.

"Do you think this is funny", he went on.

"No I don't, but if I had been killed it would have been pretty sad, but you would not have come out here", I replied.

"Do you realize that the U.S. Government is going to have to pay this man $750.00 for the dead animal, and the villagers are going to eat the animal", he asked?

"I don't really care what they do with the animal," I answered.

"I know that you don't care Lieutenant, and personally I don't like your attitude", he hammered.

With that said the Advisor and the Village Chief left. Then Capt Emrath called me to ask what the confrontation was about and I told him only to hear him laugh. Capt. Emrath told me that if it happened again to send them to him and he would tell them where to go. The man was protecting me as if I were his young cub, and I guess in a way I was. He told me I would bring up the rear the next day and second platoon with Lt. Murgia would lead. I thought that was good since I needed the break after that exhausting afternoon.

All night long the Village Chief kept heckling me about the buffalo. After they gutted and started to cook the animal, he would even come by and taunt me as he ate a rib with meat on it. He continued calling me No. 10 which in their language means the worst. I knew the confrontation between him and I was not over yet. Maybe this guy was related to the Chinese men at the meat market in Centerville, California.

That night I kept thinking how I hated the Village Chief and for a nickel more I could include the advisor in that group. The next morning as the company moved out they did it in a slow manner as they had to clear some rice paddy dikes of trip mines and other booby traps. My FO Alvin Burke pointed a hole in the ground to me that was full of fresh water. I knew it would be some time before my platoon moved out so I went to look at it. It was a round hole in the ground about six feet in depth and with about four feet of clear water.

I got my towel and soap and jumped into the hole and took a bath in the clear blue water. I was followed by Burk and SFC Rodriguez. We felt good, although the hole was now soapy on the top. We dressed and moved out with the rest of the company. About late afternoon we came upon another hamlet and Lt. Murgia made camp there. I was talking to my platoon members about setting up ambushes for the night when the same Huey from the night before landed and the Advisor and the Village Chief stepped out of the bird and headed straight toward me.

Somehow I knew I was in for another confrontation with these guys. The Captain came straight to me and in a very hostile voice asked me if I had poisoned a water well in the village we had left that morning. He turned as if apologizing to the Chief and confirmed the other man's suspicions. At which time the Chief started his finger pointing at me again and calling me by what was his common name for me of No. 10.

I was getting tired of both of these clowns and I thought that I might as well clear the air.

The Advisor turned to me and said that he could not believe that I has harassing this man in such manner and that he was going to have to pay him $750.00 more dollars and dig him a new water well. There was not much I could say so as the advisor turned to explain the gifts he was going to give to the chief, when I started to sing a Spanish song entitled *"Sabor a Mi"* and at the same time I lowered my right hand to my groin and grabbed a handful. The Chief looked at me and told the advisor that I was making fun of him by singing and doing graphic things. I told the advisor that I was a Mexican and if I chose to sing or hum in Spanish that was my choice.

As he turned to talk to the Chief, I started singing again and did the hand trick again. This infuriated the Chief as he could only guess what I was singing about but my hand motions gave him a pretty good idea. So again he ratted on me to the Advisor who turned on me like a lion and said, "I don't believe there are officers like you in the U.S. Army Lt. Villarreal". I pointed him toward Capt Emrath and told him "There is my commander over there if you have a gripe about me and my Battalion Commander is LTC James Dingeman." At that time both ninnies left.

As they left to get on the Huey I kept on singing *"Sabor a Mi"* and as the Chief looked one last time I did the hand optics again. By, By *Señores! Adios!*

CHAPTER 17

Return to Quan Loi

Well soon it was time to return to return to the Michelin Rubber Plantation. The Chinooks picked us up for a short trip to an airfield near Cu Chi where another group of Hooks would pick us up for the rest of the trip. They dropped us off at the almost abandoned airfield and soon it was time to sleep as the other Chinooks did not show and would not come until the next day. We were all dirty but there were no facilities to bathe so we made the best of the situation and went to sleep there, some of the men played cards especially John Shew and Capt Emrath.

In the morning we were woken to the noise of military jeeps surrounding the entire group. I noticed a verbal argument ensued between what appeared as armed Military Police and some of my men. I approached the angry soldiers and found out one of the MPs had used his boot to wake one of my men up. The MP said he wanted us to move because we were all dirty and Bob Hope was going to land there and the MPs did not want him to see us all dirty. When he said that one of my men named Howard picked up an M-60 and pointed it at the dressed up MPs and stood his ground. I advised the MPs that we were not moving and that if Bob Hope did not want to see real foot soldiers he could close his eyes.

Soon the Chinook landed while we still had the confrontation with the MPs and before we knew it Bob Hope, Ann Margret, Rosy Greer and a group of beautiful girls named the Gold Diggers were among us. Pandemonium set in as the men pulled out cameras and took pictures, some lucky ones even got a kiss from Ann Margret and the Gold Diggers. I think it was the MP and not Bob Hope that wanted us out of there.

CHAPTER 18

Christmas in the boonies

It was beginning to be Christmas in the boonies and we received word of a Christmas seize fire for twenty four hours. My question was could we trust the enemy to abide by the terms of the seize fire. Any way we received a Christmas menu from the Battalion Commander and Christmas cards from the Cavalry to send home. The menu said we were going to have all the goodies as if we were home, but we new that the Santa around here did not arrive in a sleight and most likely would have fixed bayonets instead of jingle bells. We would have to make the most of a bad situation. I wondered how the turkey and mashed potatoes and all the other goodies would taste drooped from several hundred feet in artillery containers and slammed into the earth.

Well, Christmas in the jungle arrived and we experienced our twenty four hour cease fire. Everything started smoothly and the Hueys dropped our long expected Holiday meal. All the goodies the Battalion Commander had promised arrived and yes they were a bit damaged from the fall but for hungry Cav troopers, it was food from heaven. We ate everything and kept on eating into the afternoon until all the pies and fruits were gone.

Now, it was time to rest for a few hours and wait for the cease fire to end and to see what would happen next. At about four o'clock in the after noon, I sent my ambush out with instructions not to fire until after six. About five in the afternoon the NCO in charge of the ambush called that an enemy patrol had come out of the jungle and was heading toward Quan Loi when they stopped and appeared to be having lunch and partying around. He wanted instructions, and I advised him to wait another hour after the cease fire and then engage.

The hour went by slowly and I was hoping the enemy patrol was still there and having a good time. Well, it was a hard decision to make, but I told them to engage and move back to our location.

As darkness crept on, the shooting started and it was over quickly. Soon our patrol finished their engagement and returned to our location. I did not really want the stats and told the men to settle back and relax. I often wonder whether the enemy even knew about the cease fire or whether they even had a watch, someone said once, "war is hell" and this was a good example.

We continued working around Quan Loi but we could tell that the enemy patrols were more numerous as we approached the Lunar New Year or Tet. Yes, the enemy was getting ready on their march on Saigon to celebrate their New Year. The next few months would go down as the Tet Offensive of 1969.

Capt. Emrath was given a staff job at the 2-12th TOC and he would be joining LTC Dingeman, Major Billy Brown, Lt. Tripp, and Lonnie Murdock on the staff. I would assume command until we received a new commander. One day shortly after the New Year, a Huey came in with supplies I was called to go toward the supply bird as the new commander was coming in.

When I arrived and stretched my hand at the new CO, I realized that I knew him from Ft. Benning. "Hello Lt. Villarreal, remember me"? There standing in front of me was Capt. James Graham the tactics instructor from OCS. I was very happy to get a well rounded and experienced commander of the caliber of Capt. Graham. LTC Dingeman had not come to make the change in commands, because when he had mentioned I was in charge of the company, Capt Graham told him he already knew me. "Lt Villarreal, we are going to get along just fine", he said. I knew we would get along great. And we did and for the next several months I realized what a true leader this man was.

Chapter 19

Capt. James Graham at the helm.

We were now under the leadership of Capt. Graham a middle age prior service officer who knew what he was doing. Working under him was like driving a new Cadillac, everything seemed smooth and with a purpose. One day working in the Michelin I was doing search and destroy with my platoon when I strayed from the company and had to settle for the night under the rubber trees. I stumbled into a platoon of tanks and we settle in together for the evening.

Upon settling in I noticed the platoon leader for the tank unit kept looking at me and I wondered why. Upon giving him a closer look I realized it was Lt. Michael V. Lloyd one of the TACs from my OCS company. He was platoon leader in a tank company with the 1st Infantry Division. At first I was kind of withdrawn because I still remembered this man yelling and giving us hell at OCS. Now he was a peer and seemed very much down to earth, a side I had not seen at OCS. We chatted most of the night as we camped together. We were glad to be in company of the tanks and they were of the ground infantry.

Bright and early next morning we were getting up when there was a big explosion on a rubber tree near one of the tanks, as an enemy soldier had fired a rocket at it. Like lighting the tanks sprung into action charging the enemy who were dug in a wood line outside the rubber trees. Like a flash it started and the tanks went into motion firing their machineguns and their big guns. They rolled over the enemy position and never stopped nor looked back. They left us exploiting the remains of the enemy position and we never saw them again. There were dead NVA (North Vietnamese Soldiers) in the temporary dugouts most of them shot many times and then squashed by the tanks. I did not get to see Lt. Lloyd again as the tanks disappeared into the rubber plantation. I reported to Capt Graham my encounter with the friendly unit and the little action we had seen.

We kept moving and in the direction of the Cambodian Border. We ran into a platoon of the 11th Armor Cav. These were not tanks but mounted Armor personnel carriers and very much like the tanks they struck like lightning. Again we had a couple of skirmishes but the armor quickly pacified the situation with their lightning speed and many weapons.

We continued thru the jungle occasionally coming up either a main trail or a small road. I started to follow a road that showed signs of heavy use, when suddenly I noticed there was heavy displays of bamboo stakes sharp and pointed toward the trail. This was usually a sign an ambush was near and usually on the opposite side of the road so they could push us into the bamboo stakes with their gunfire. I quickly sensed that we were on an ambush. I singled for Sgt. Griffin to bring up his M-60 and spray the area to our right front. This quickly brought a response from the enemy who were dug in bunkers to our right front.

All of a sudden we were in the middle of a firefight with Sgt Griffin and his gunner and I in front of the column and the rest of the men behind us and for the most part unable to shoot. Sgt Griffin had just returned from the states from visiting his new born baby girl. He was still a bit shaken from the long trip to paradise and his now quick immersion into combat again.

I realized most of the enemy fire was coming from a bunker directly in front of us. I grabbed a grenade from my chest and gave it to SGT Griffin and told him to take the bunker out. I did this like a greenhorn platoon leader which I was not any longer. All of a sudden SGT Griffin looked at me and offered the grenade back and said "You want to show me how 1-6." In a world of men in combat I new that the challenge was in my court and I had to show my stuff or lose the respect of this NCO and probably the rest of the men. I executed the slowest and closest to the ground low crawl I had ever done. Now I was but a couple of meters away from the bunker and could see the barrel of the machinegun coming out of the opening.

I pulled the pin and even with the experience in combat I now had, my heart was in my throat and several other parts of my body seemed in the wrong place. I held it for several seconds after the pin flew out and threw it right into the opening. There was a loud explosion and somehow I stood up and emptied my Carbine into the bunker (that's what John Wayne would have done).

SGT Griffin came up and cleared the bunker as I sat there exhausted. The crisis was over but I was drained of energy. The unit advanced thru the enemy ambush and I realized that SGT Griffin had taught me a lesson about leadership and that was that sometimes you have to lead by example. We were on the move again as the enemy patrols seemed to be more numerous when one day I was near the front of the unit and came under heavy small arms fire. I reported to Capt Graham that I was unable to advance or retreat.

The third platoon was under the leadership of a big negro NCO named Dawson as Lt. Shlifka the platoon leader had rotated back to the U.S. Actually Lt. Murgia had rotated also and 2nd platoon did not have a platoon leader either. Here I was behind a log unable to move when an enemy soldier had tried to rush and shoot me as I laid there behind the long but I had been faster on the trigger and now he was on the other side of the log dead. All of a sudden I hear this commotion as SFC Dawson was coming to my rescue and he was yelling "Here I come 1-6, I'll get you out". He had a grenade in his hand which he lobed at the enemy who were real close.

He dropped to the ground in front of me and said "I got them little rascals 1-6, but I think they got me too". Well in reality the grenade he threw had landed so close to all of us a piece had hit him in the tummy. SFC Dawson was a combat veteran on his second tour and he made his presence felt as he was one big fellow. Thanks SFC Dawson, for he had sprung me loose from the enemy that had me pinned down at such a close proximity.

The next day we continue our move and somehow I was still in the lead. My point man that day was a new man named David Henier. The point man had a dog handler that I only remember as Pancho and a beautiful black German Sheppard dog named "Ilo". David called me to show all the activity on the trail as Pancho held on to his dog who was being very active denoting the presence of the enemy. All of a sudden I heard talking and looked up only to find two NVA soldiers walking together at right shoulder arms smiling. When they saw me they froze in place and I emptied my Car-15 at both. As they went down all hell broke loose to our front and David Heiner was injured.

At that time "Ilo" was charging to the front as if protecting David when Pancho was grazed on the forehead by a bullet. Now, I had David and Pancho wounded and down and the dog raising hell to attack the enemy. I signaled for SSG John Perkins to bring Walter Hoxworth with his M-60. Hoxworth came charging up as if possessed by a super being firing on fully automatic and covering everything to our front. Walter Hoxworth was a master with the M.60 and a sight to see when he engaged the enemy. I remember that he had a small speech impediment but it did not affect his ability to make the machine gun sing. As he fired I was able to retrieve Heiner and later returned to retrieve Pancho. That dog gave me hell since his handler was unconscious and he wanted to attack the gooks.

It seemed to me we had stumbled into a nest of NVA with those first two going out to a listening post or something. I knew I would never get another opportunity for some easy and quick kills. I rounded up the men and with our wounded in tow we left the area. Heiner recovered and came back later, Pancho I never saw again but I did get word that he had recovered later. (Several months later I received a Bronze Star with "V" for that day).

CHAPTER 20

MadMex and the Rice

Well our Battalion Commander LTC Dingeman was getting ready to rotate and soon we would have a new Commander. Meanwhile it was decided that we were working so close to an abandoned French Fort we might as well move the battalion(2ⁿᵈ 12ᵗʰ Cav) and two artillery batteries, one of 105 Howitzers and one of 155 Howitzers there. This was mostly to give us the coverage of the artillery and we could exploit the jungles around the Michelin and on toward the Cambodian Border. I had never seen the artillery up close, but to see these young men working a fire mission up close was great. I learned to like and respect these so-called red legs and I got to see them die just like our infantry guys.

Picture of the young artillerymen at LZ Grant firing a fire mission.

Along with the artillery we made that old fort our new home. It had the name of LZ Grant and eventually would go down as one of the hot spots of the war. One Infantry Company would provide security for the Landing Zone and the artillery and our staff while three infantry companies would work the surrounding area. The Recon Company would do special missions for the Commander also around the area.

LZ Grant was like an oblong fat French bread in shape. One of the tips was facing a dirt road coming from Tay Ninh while the other overlooked an old metal bridge that was straddled over the river (stream). At or below the bridge there was a water hole which quickly became our water point. Of course the road from Tay Ninh was now blocked by LZ Grant. On the way to the water point stood the remains of the Old French Fort facing the ghostly frame of the bridge. I guess the French soldiers would control the use and traffic of the bridge from the old fort.

Some us did not feel the impact of the move as we continued working like we had without too much change except maybe move a little closer to Grant to utilize the fire support from the artillery. We were not selected to be the first unit at Grant therefore we did not have to clear the old berm nor did we have to build the new bunkers. Somewhere during this time LTC James Dingeman rotated and a new commander by the name of LTC Peter Gorvad became our commander. The rest of the staff remained the same at the TOC. We still had Major Billy Brown, Capt Emrath, Lt. Tripp and SSG Lonnie Murdock.

I am standing at the fifty caliber position
overlooking the water point at LZ Grant.

Harold Hopper, Hoss Parrish and another platoon member
overlooking the old French Fort. at Grant.

LZ Grant had twenty four bunkers that were usually manned by three to four men depending on our numbers. I usually got the six bunkers overlooking the old French fort and therefore the water point. Here on these bunkers the land was mostly downhill as it led toward the river. It was one of the easiest places to get close to the artillery guns by the enemy since the land gave way toward the river. The enemy found it easy to crawl to the old fort and from there began firing upon our bunkers but mostly upon the artillery guns behind us a few meters. It was also easy for the artillery to lower the guns and blast them behind the old cement walls. Also the quad fifty mounted on the army truck was not very effective because the terrain was not level.

Every morning my men would accompany the combat engineers to clear the road leading to the water point of land mines placed during the night by our little friends. Even clearing every day there were some accidents as a vehicle would set off a mine. One day the third platoon was enjoying bathing and playing water games at the water point when Capt Graham ask me to get them out and take my platoon to relax in the water for a while. I approached the men and in my usual calm manner asked them to get out so that my men could cool off. They ignored me completely and went on playing.

After several attempts to oust them from the river to no avail, I pulled a grenade from my shirt and pulled the pin. At this time there was complete silence as the men looked at me in disbelief. Once I had their attention I threw the grenade into the water and before the five seconds elapsed and the explosion could be heard all the men were running up the hill toward LZ Grant completely naked and carrying their gear. They were met by LTC Gorvad and Capt. Graham who were coming to inspect the water point. One of the men yelled at the officers "That is one crazy mad Mexican down there". LTC Gorvad asked Capt Graham, "I wondered what happened down there".

"Well, I sent Lt. Villarreal to rotate the men at the river and he has his way of motivating people". Sometime later someone threw a grenade with the pin still in at the Mortar Platoon and although no one said anything I know that some wondered whether I had thrown it, but all they had to do was ask me. After the water point incident I picked up the nickname "Mad-Mex"

Our Mortar Platoon on a fire mission.

Upon leaving Grant we moved past the old bridge and went a couple of kilometers when my point man called me to the front to show me a trail that crossed the main road. The trail came from the direction of Cambodia and headed south in the general direction of Saigon but mostly it seemed to me it was paralleling the river we were blocking at Grant. I could see a lot of bicycle tracks and some Ho Chi Min slicks on the ground. We followed the trail south and found a cave with new bicycles still with the price tags on them as Christmas specials in the U.S. Some of the men were upset at this since they realized someone was helping these rascals buy American made bicycles. It did get us into the military newspapers but the hurt was still there.

I am giving my Car.15 a little dusting before night fall at LZ Grant.

The next day we encountered two *gooks* riding the same type of bicycles and captured them. We started to investigate them and found them sort of uncooperative. A couple of the men and our company medic Patrick Shertzer personally got involved in interrogating the prisoners. What our men found out was that there was a camp on the other side of the road or toward Cambodia from where we were working. That was the direction these enemy soldiers were coming from. The date of this incident was January 30, 1969.

As we proceeded we covered both sides of the trail as not to miss anything that might help find the camp. As we proceeded we came under intense enemy small arms and rocket fire from the front or toward Cambodia. One of our men was hit by a rocket direct fire and there was not much left of him to save (PFC Carl Joseph Andrus). I remember the look on Jeffrey Spencer and another soldier as they went by with his body in a poncho. We were also receiving men who were being shot in the back which only meant that the enemy was in the trees. I had all the men clear each tree by firing from the bottom to the top of the trees. Soon enemy snipers were falling to the ground and it stopped our men from being shot in the back.

SGT. Rex Gordon (Skarky) and Patrick Shertzer sipping
a beer with two other soldiers at LZ Grant.

Again the firing started from the front of our column and we had a
fight on our hands. Capt Graham requested air support as our artillery
batteries were hammering away but we needed more. As the jets dove
into where we suspected the enemy to be, they reported white foam like
material flying as the bombs exploded. We found out what it was when
the enemy was taken care of and it was tons and tons of rice. We had
captured the biggest rice cache of the Viet-Nam War. The rice was in
one hundred kilo bags and piled very high. What I personally counted
was about two hundred tons, later it was estimated at one hundred
tons.

We had just captured the rice that the enemy was going to use as
food during their offensive on Saigon during TET 69. Capt. Graham
was elated with the find and the Battalion Commander was seen
showing the rice to the high officers of the Cavalry. They all came to
get their pictures taken with the rice we had captured. Our reward was
that at night we would boil some of the rice to add to our C-Rations.
It was a great feeling to be involved in the capture of the rice although
we had paid a price for it.

Shortly after the rice find we were given a two day break at Tay Ninh
where we were able to shower with real clean water, we got a change of

clothes and some good food to include shrimp cocktails. From somewhere Capt Graham appeared with two "Donut Dollies" to entertain the men. Capt. Graham was always trying to cheer the men up and he was a master at that. I was able to call Linda after standing in line half the night. It was a well deserved reward for the men that had fought hard and had carried the rice to the Chinooks to be hauled away.

Capt James Graham with two "Donut Dollies"
at our two day break in Tay Ninth.

Well, we returned to work our area of operations and one night I took my platoon on an ambush to the outskirts of the Michelin. We settled down on an "L" shaped ambush sight facing a road coming out of the jungle and into the rubber plantation. I had the two machine guns in place and set out some claymores. These claymores had made a believer out of me since they were so effective as long as they were braced against a rubber tree and would go full blast toward the front and not harm anyone behind them. All the men were hidden in the shadows created by the big rubber trees.

The men were pretty tired so I placed them in groups of three so that two could rest while one out of every group could watch. About midnight I was resting when I heard a voice in Spanish say *"Wake up*

Vic, they are coming", I woke up and looked around my ambush and everyone of my lookouts had also fallen asleep, everyone was sleeping. Still curious of who had woken me up I looked toward the kill zone and saw a large group of enemy soldiers in it. My first thought was that if everyone was sleeping to let the enemy go. Then I remembered a trip flare we had put across the road to illuminated the kill zone.

The lead man was about to trip it and then hell would break loose. I looked at the lead man and when he was about to trip the flare he looked toward me and smiled. I looked at his face and even saw it was green from the moonlight, I could see his frightened look of death all over his face. I had no choice but to click the switch on the claymores and all of a sudden my men all woke up firing on fully automatic and mowing down the enemy patrol. Boy, that had been a close call, and to this date I don't know who woke me up but I am very thankful for that voice.

Hoss Parrish moving a huge bag of rice as Rubadeu looks on.

Water Point at LZ Grant

Lt. Vic Villarreal digging foxhole and doing foot care.

Chapter 21

Meet Father Hugh Black

The rice was extracted and taken to Tay Ninh to be distributed to the poor people in the area. We wondered how much of the rice would end in the hands of the enemy again. And so we moved further away or closer toward the Cambodian Border. One evening a Huey came in as I was preparing to go on ambush with one of my squads while SFC Rodriguez would remain with the other squad on the perimeter. At this time I was the only other officer besides Capt Graham. The Huey landed and supplies were unloaded as well as our Battalion Chaplain. The Chaplain was a catholic priest by the name of Hugh Black and he had been with us for some time as we traveled in our area of operations.

The best way to describe this man was that he was a tall, blue eyed, handsome man in his thirties. He was always smiling and making us feel good. Tonight was no exception except that he had a message from the Battalion Commander for us. He asked for all the minorities to meet with him on one side of the perimeter so he could deliver the message from LTC Gorvad. He started by saying that the commander was concerned that some of the minorities with in the ranks were being treated unfairly or had even seen some discrimination from superiors. It was getting dark and he could not see us correctly when we burst out laughing.

Father Hugh Black having a chat with company
RTO John Shew from NYC.

He became concerned with this outburst and wanted to know why.
One of the men told him that most of us were minorities including
the only other officer in the unit (me)and several of the higher ranking
NCOs like Rodriguez and Dawson. At this time he became very relaxed
and decided to go with us on ambush, he was what we called very gun
ho for a man carrying a bible.

We were late and unable to dig our foxholes, so we made the best of
a bad situation. The Padre stayed with me and the radio operator, who
was Hopper, at that time. As luck would have it the men spotted a large
enemy patrol headed for our kill zone. As they approached, I set off the
claymores and the men opened up with the small arms fire. I looked at
the Padre after the confrontation as he laid on the ground and he was
very pale, as it was his complexion was very light, but now, he was white

and I could only imagine what he was thinking. It was over quickly and we gathered the spoils of war and retreated to our main camp.

In the morning Father Black went about his business of giving mass and taking confessions. At that time Hopper told me that LTC Gorvad wanted me on the radio. He asked for a report of the ambush and I told him we had encountered an enemy patrol that numbered at least eighteen and that we had killed at least three with many blood trials visible and had captured 7 AK 47s.

He stopped to think and said that it did not add up. He repeated, three bodies and 7 weapons do not add to at least eighteen. At that I laughed and told him we had also captured eighteen sets of Ho Chi Min slicks all pointing toward the place I had set off the claymores at the beginning of the ambush. The enemy would usually fly out of their "slicks" when confronted by an explosion or gunfire. He laughed and I told him I would send them in with the weapons on the Padre's chopper. He wanted to know one more question, "Did you take the Padre on the ambush?"

I answered, "Yes" and he had no reply. Losing Father Black was inconceivable to all of us since he brought us together and kept us going in our beliefs when we were confronted by such obstacles in this war. Keeping Father Black from doing what he wanted to do was also inconceivable. He was considered a gutsy person by all the men. They often made combat cartoons about him carrying an M-60 in one hand, a grenade on the other and a bowie knife in the grip of his teeth. I hope he was not offended by the gestures of the men, but the bottom line was that everybody loved Father Black.

CHAPTER 22

The Jerry Moore Story

In the middle of February I left the company near the Cambodian Border to go to An Khe to pick up the company payroll. Some how I got over there by riding in a small plane called the Caribou. When I left the company it had been slow for a few days but I still hated leaving the Commander alone without any other officer. The good thing was that SFC Dawson had returned and SFC Rodriguez was there also. They both had a lot of combat experience and would support the Capt in any situation

I picked up the payroll which consisted a several thousands of dollars in MPC (MPC was really play money that was issued so that the soldiers would not spend real U.S. Dollars in the economy and the enemy would not get their hands on it to use in the Black Market). Usually a soldier would only receive a fraction of his earnings and send the rest home automatically. I also picked up some booze that the men had asked me to bring back especially Al Burk who loved that Johnny Red.

I was really loaded down and had problem getting back to Tay Ninh. When I got to Cam Ranh Bay I did not have a way to get to Saigon so I hopped an Air Force Medical Plane. The pilot was a female Major and did not want me on board because I was armed. The plane was loaded with ROKs or Korean mercenaries that had been wounded and were being sent back to Korea but had to be checked out in Saigon first. In Saigon I missed my flight to Tay Ninh and had to spend the night in the middle of the city with an MP who was escorting a black soldier who had deserted.

It was a long night as we sat there, the sergeant watching his prisoner and I watching the government payroll. We talked about going home and before we knew it we dozed off and I woke up to find my payroll safe but the prisoner had escaped. I woke up the sergeant and told him his prisoner was gone. He went into a panic and ran down the stairs of the cheap hotel looking for him. He was not able to find him and knew he was going to be in trouble, I was thankful the man had not taken the payroll.

We sat there looking at each other when the door opened and the prisoner came in accompanied by two girls and loaded down with Chinese food. He put the food down and walked over to where he had taken the handcuffs and put them back on. How, about that, he had returned on his own. He asked the sergeant if the two girls could stay with him until we left in the morning. We were confused until he explained that he got hungry during the night, had taken the cuffs off and gone looking for food. He had run across two of his favorite girls from a club he ran while he had been absent without official leave in the street below. He had borrowed some money from them to bring us food since he knew we had not eaten.

We were glad he had returned and gave him permission to be with his girls until we left in the morning. No one slept the rest of the night. In the morning he ran the women off and we took a cab to the airport to hitch a ride. I was able to get to Tay Ninh and to my unit headquarters to look for a chopper to take me back to Charlie Company.

I was advised that my unit had been in contact with the enemy all morning and Capt. Graham was anxious to have me back.

I departed in a Huey with my payroll and bag with the booze. I was taken straight to the company perimeter and again advised that they were under fire. The pilots of the Huey said they could go in under fire but I would be dropped off and then they would leave the area. As the Huey approached the company perimeter and we were but twenty feet or so off the ground we began to take incoming rounds.

As the bird approached an open area to land the door gunners started firing back at the enemy. I was told to get ready to get off. As I looked out the Huey side door I saw two NVA soldiers carrying an

American black soldier by both arms. He appeared to be wounded, because it looked like he was unconscious. I drew my Car-15 to kill the NVA but because of the vibrations of the Huey I was not sure I would not hit the American soldier. They disappeared into the trees and heavy vegetation and that was the last I saw of them.

I quickly jumped out off the Huey and ran for cover as bullets were flying everywhere. The chopper took off and disappeared being followed by the enemy gunfire. I asked the soldiers on the ground where Capt. Graham was located and they pointed toward a spot in the jungle. I headed in that direction and quickly found the company command post. What I saw was not very encouraging.

I looked and Capt. Graham was sitting and directing air and artillery strikes against the enemy. That was my commander always in charge and fighting back. Next to him was a dead soldier that I recognized as SGT. John Pinney whom I had seen around the company before but not in my platoon. Even in death Sgt Pinney looked like a big young man. Next to Pinney was the Radio Operator wounded in one eye and clamoring about his wounds. I dropped the payroll and bag of booze and sat next to Capt. Graham.

I told the Commander that I was back and what instructions he had for me. He looked at me with a blank look on his face and I could see blood running from his eyebrows.

"Vic, I'm blind" he said." I don't want the men to know because we might have a panic on our hands" he continued.

"I understand that one new man that came in earlier already panicked and the enemy captured him" he added. "Try to organize the company and get us out of here" was his command. "Do just what you did at Ft. Benning on the practical exercise" he instructed.

I knew I had a big challenge in front of me because the commander was blind, I had a dead soldier on our hands and the wounded to take with us including the radio operator. Unknown to me was that SFC Dawson had been wounded pretty seriously and several others including a new officer (Lt. Rick Kopec) was also wounded. And there was the missing soldier situation.

"O.K Vic, settle down and think of a course of action", I thought to myself I gathered the dead and wounded to a central location and got the company ready to move out. I had SFC Rodriguez look for an opening in the enemy positions and we got ready to move out in that direction. With both batteries of artillery at LZ Grant pounding away we moved out in the direction of Grant. SFC Rodriguez in all his experience and wise moves had picked the right break in the enemy positions. I had the artillery halt for a while and the ARA gun ships took over as we moved out smartly and they escorted us with both rocket and mini guns blazing. There were a lot of H.E rounds of both artillery and from the gun ships expanded that afternoon.

We went several clicks away and I was able to get a Huey in to pick up the dead and wounded. I had lost PFC Moore for the time being, and the next decision was hard to make. I called LTC Gorvad and informed him that Capt. Graham was on his way in a med-a-vac as were the other wounded and SGT Pinney's body. I told him to let the B-52s rip the area and then have the Cobras finish whatever was left of the enemy. Hueys with loud speakers came out and were calling for Jerry Moore to move to a location where he could get picked up. He was never seen again.

That evening Bad Bet or B-2-12th met up with us to reinforce our company for the exploitation of the battle area and the search for PFC Moore. Unfortunately we never found PFC Gerry Moore.

This has been one of several incidents that still plague my mind. Capt. Graham never returned to the company and I took command for the second time. Even thought I was twenty-one I felt that I was over forty years old.

In all the confusion I did not know that a new officer by the name of Rick Kopec had joined the company the day before in the heat of contact. He had come in an earlier chopper along with PFC Gerry Moore and been wounded on his first day. Lt. Kopec would turn out to be a great asset to the company and a very good friend to me. Later when the going got tough he proved to me I could depend on him and he had no shortage of guts. (The time of the year was February 16 and 17th of 1969).

CHAPTER 23

Harold Hopper meets the Snake

Harold (Bill) Hopper was my RTO (Radio Operator) during those first months of TET 69 and a more sincere man you could not ask for. He was a man who carried the radio for me under the most difficult situations and would not back down from a good fight with the enemy. He kept me informed of everything going on the radio and he also got along very well with the Artillery FO Alvin Burk. Usually while I was trying to assessed the situation he would cover my back very well. One day a sniper was taking pot shots at me and Bill could not shoot him off a tree where the sniper was hidden, so he asked me to get him an M-14 rifle which fired a heavier round and from that day on he was shooting the snipers as if they were fat turkeys in the trees back home.

After numerous fire fights I knew what he could do and that was everything required of him. At night fall he was the first to prepare the foxhole. Of course Alvin would help him and SFC Rodriguez and I would do our part. Between the four we could defend ourselves well in case of a firefight and I knew that we could depend on one another in case the enemy tried to overrun our positions.

Picture of Harold Hopper on left, I in the middle, Parrish
next to me, California Don and Kenny Covington. Kneeling
is SFC Rodriguez two other soldiers in the picture.

One day we were humping the boonies and it was very hot. The sun
was beating on us to where we were drinking a lot of water. We were
sweating profusely so I decided to stop for the day. As we started to dig
in the ground was very hard and we were having problems advancing
with our foxholes. Our particular foxhole was at the base of a large
bamboo group. The bamboo stalks were about two inches in diameter
and about twenty feet in height.

Suddenly Hopper stood up and grabbed one of the bamboo stalks
only to yell out in pain. When he grabbed the stalk he accidentally put
his hand on a bamboo viper perhaps one of the most deadly snakes in
Viet-Nam. The Bamboo viper is about fifteen inches in length and a
waning green color and almost impossible to detect. He was pinning

the snake onto the bamboo so the snake just turned its head and bit him on the hand.

He yelled out and I came over and killed the snake, however Bill was down on the ground and very pale. I summoned a med-a-vac and Hopper was quickly picked up but he was already losing it. He began to drift off in to unconsciousness and going into shock. I was very concerned for my faithful radio operator, but mostly I was concerned for the life of my friend Harold(Bill) Hopper. You always figure that you lose a soldier with his guns blazing, not bitten by a silly little deadly snake.

I did not hear from him or of him until a few years ago when I found him living with his family in Alabama. Bill had not changed one bit. He was still a great and sincere person just like he was during the war. I hope he never changes.

CHAPTER 24

LZ Grant under attack.

The tour of duty at LZ Grant would prove to be a tough one. The LZ was on very strategic ground that the North Vietnamese Army needed for their approach on Saigon for the TET Offensive of 1969. They were willing to spend men and resources to secure this precious ground. The following months were going to test the fiber and grit of the 1st Cavalry Sky Troopers in the attempts to keep LZ Grant in U.S. possession. Many lives were going to be lost on both sides to keep this sacred ground. The river that ran next to the LZ was going to run red with blood of men from both sides fighting to keep the upper hand in the balance of power.

Commanders and soldiers on both sides would try to prove whose testorone would prevail. The history books say that there were three battles fought for control of LZ Grant. Those of us that were there know that there were four battles fought in the spring of 69 (TET 69) and some men lost their lives in proof of the fourth battle that somehow got lost in the writings of the battles. I will reconstruct the fourth battle to the best of my ability in honor of the men that lost their lives and limbs to protect that sacred ground. In writing about the fourth battle I will refer to a letter from the Internet written by another veteran of the action Jeffery Spenzer from Avon Lake, Ohio, a member of the Second Platoon, Charlie Company, Second of the 12th Cavalry.

CHAPTER 25

The first attack came on
February 23 1969.

The first major attempt at LZ Grant came on Feb. 23, 1969 and smack in the TET Offensive. We may ask why a major attack on this lonely dusty piece of Viet-Nam real estate? Well the old French Fort had been there since the French War in Indochina. It was on most maps that were issued to the NVA commanders. It was easy to obtain the grid coordinates to zero the rocket and mortar attacks. It was also on a main road and a permanent bridge next to the old French Fort. LZ Grant was straddled on the road and also blocking the river which was a major water supply for the troops moving in on Saigon. Also the Commies had their rice and weapons caches along the river as was proven by the many tons of rice that we had captured. There was also evidence of large bunker complexes along the river which served the enemy as hospitals for their wounded in the up coming battles.

LZ Grant was like a pearl in the eyes of the NVA commanders. It was a morsel that was tempting to the eye and the overrunning of this American post could mean some promotion for a North Vietnamese General. LZ Grant had to be taken out in the eyes of the enemy. The enemy was not counting on a stubborn group of Americans that made up the Roving Gambler Battalion and this evening it was B Company(Bad Bet). This company of determined soldiers would lose one man killed (SGT Bobby Sanderson)

There were also two, very determined artillery batteries, that weren't going to just give up, not as long as there were bullets and artillery rounds to shoot at the enemy. From the commanders down to the last infantry rifleman and artillery gunner they all knew the mission which was to hold the landing zone against all odds.

The North Vietnamese normally attack in three waves. The first wave is fully armed and made up of their top soldiers. The second wave, is only armed every other man, as those unarmed go forward looking for a fallen weapons with live ammo. The third, wave are their inferior warriors who for the most part don't have a weapon of their own and have to depend on a fallen comrade or American to get a weapon. This wave is the one that is the most fun to shoot since, they really want to fight but don't have the weapons to do so.

The defenders of LZ Grant were basically the same ones for all of the attacks on the base except that the ground infantry companies rotated. The ground infantry units were elements of 2nd of the 12 Cavalry which consisted of the Headquarters Company and E Company (Recon) plus one of the infantry line companies of the 2nd of the 12 Cav. The Battalion commander would utilize one of the four infantry companies plus the Recon Company to secure the perimeter and patrol outside the perimeter during the day to keep the *gooks* from getting too close to the berm. The other three companies would clover leaf in their search and destroy maneuvers, trying to keep the NVA on the run.

There were two artillery units also assigned to LZ Grant. One Battery consisted of 155s artillery guns (1/30 FA) while the other battery was 105 artillery guns (2/19 FA). These artillerymen were well trained and very gutsy individuals as they proved it time and time again. On February 23, 1969 both the infantry and the artillery troops were ready to defend LZ Grant. A battery would suffer two wounded and one man killed that night. CPL Jesse B. Montez was killed that evening and like many other red legs that were killed later, he never abandoned his gun, and kept on firing under the worst conditions.

The artillery men of the 155 battery were able to expend almost six hundred rounds and many rounds were fired in direct fire role. They were credited with 13 enemy kills but no telling what the actual count was since the enemy usually carried their dead to bury somewhere else and deny the Americans the satisfaction of the kills.

Chapter 26

The Second Attack on March 08, 1969

The attack on March 8, 1969 was a costly one as the 2Bn 12th Cav took ten KIAs and many wounded and the Artillery had 4 KIAs that night. .The NVA Regiment that had surrounded LZ Grant started their attack with a rocket and mortar attack on the Landing Zone. They started with an enemy sniper who fired one round, the round that killed Lt. Grant H. Henjyoji the Platoon Leader that had replaced me on my sector overlooking the French Fort, and the water plant.

I had met Lt. Heniyoji that same afternoon as we were given the order by LTC Gorvad to move out and that we would be replaced by D Company (Double Deuce). I met him in my bunker sector as he wanted to know his area of responsibility and the number of bunkers he was responsible for. It seemed to me that here was a very nice young man trying his best to do the right thing. I told him the weaknesses of the location we had to cover, which was that the enemy would crawl in the area between the water point and the Old French Fort and embed them selves in the walls of the fort and it would take the artillery guns to blast them out and sometimes it took many rounds to do so.

John Bailey and Joe Rubadeu at LZ Grant.

As we were leaving SGT. Walter Hoxworth approached me and reminded me that the next day was his last day in the field and wanted to know weather he could stay at LZ Grant or go with us and come back the next morning. He was all excited because he was going to leave the Army and go to Australia and marry a girl he had met while on R&R. Walter had a speech impediment but he made his point clear that he wanted to stay. I embraced the good soldier and he said his goodbyes to his friends and stayed behind at Grant. He stayed at the bunker by the gate to the Huey pad and picked up an M-60 for his last night in harms way.

When we left LZ Grant we were either lucky or the enemy let us get thru them so that we could leave because the LZ was already surrounded by hundreds of enemy soldiers. We went about two clicks (kilometers) and it got dark, so Capt Brittingham, our new commander gave orders to dig in. Something did not feel right, there was a stillness in the air that could only mean an enemy attack We dug in as best we could and awaited the nightfall.

About midnight we heard the incoming rockets toward LZ Grant and the small arms fire started until it was a continuous roar of small arms, mortars and rockets combined. We knew that hell had broken loose at the landing zone. Our own artillery could be heard firing at will round after round. There was basically nothing we could do except wait till morning. And as morning came we set up ambushes as we knew that the enemy would be retreating our way because we were in the direction of the Black Virgin Mountain (Nu Ba Diem).

And they came in small groups most of them running and a lot of them either unarmed or without ammo for their weapons. They ran into our ambushes and died there without going any further. The Cobra gun ships were also racking the area for enemy trying to out run the artillery guns from Grant which were following them as they ran for cover utilizing the jungles. After the firing stopped and the enemy stop coming we got word from Grant, and it was not good.

LTC Peter Gorvad had been killed by one of the first rockets as most of his staff. Capt William R. Black the commander for Company D. was also dead as Capt John Philip Emrath my old commander Also dead were Lt. Peter Tripp whom I had replaced at Charlie Company and Lt. Grant Henijyoji the platoon Leader that had replaced me on the perimeter. The biggest shock was that Sgt Walter Hoxworth my M-60 gunner was dead and four other enlisted men on the perimeter (Larry Evans, and Charles D. Snyder were among the dead). The Recon Company had also lost two men Vincent Guerrero and John Hornsby. Upon hearing of Hoxworth's death my men sat down and started crying and I joined them. I thought if I had brought him with us he would still be alive. The feelings got worst when we found out he was killed by friendly fire.

Our friends in the artillery had also lost four dead (Thomas J. Roach, Glenn R. Stair, Roy D. Wimmer, and Gordon C. Murray). Those brave young men that would continue to fire their artillery pieces while they were receiving many incoming had had their losses too. So, the battle to keep LZ Grant open on the NVA supply route had been a costly one. It was not comforting to find out that there were twenty-eight dead NVA in front of Hoxworth's machine gun. He had gone down mowing the enemy with his M-60, when that napalm bomb from a friendly jet bounced off the concertina wire right into their bunker position burning everyone. The word I received that day was that two hundred and ninety-five NVA had been killed at Grant or around

Grant. The Artillery had had their share in the blasting of the enemy and so had Zorba the Greek our quad-50 man.

That was no way for Hoxworth to have died, he was an American soldier, a hero in anybody's book. I will always remember that muscle bound, blond young man coming to my rescue firing his M-60 as he advanced toward my position and to rescue Heiner, Pancho and I.

Rest in peace my friend.

My friend Major Billy Brown had survived the rocket that had hit the TOC (Tactical Operations Center). Apparently he was out checking the perimeter defenses when it happened. SFC Lonnie Murdock also survived the blast somehow but was seriously injured since he was inside the TOC when the rocket went off.

CHAPTER 27

The third attack came
on March ll-12, 1969

The third attack on LZ Grant would come on the evening of March 11 and go on till the next day March 12, 1969. It is apparent that there were many enemy solders in the area of Grant, perhaps because of the so-called failed attempt on Saigon. The finding of the weapons and rice caches by our units in the area might have confused or disoriented the enemy about their forward progress on the Capital. Instead they massed their forces and concentrated their efforts on nearby targets. Grant was among those targets.

LZ Grant was one target that the enemy had not destroyed, and so they turned their anger on it. Those artillery guns at Grant kept hammering the enemy with barrage after barrage of artillery rounds. You have to be close to the artillery incoming rounds to understand that it is a horrible thing to be on the receiving end of those guns. The enemy must have dug deep into their bunkers to stay alive.

This attack on LZ Grant proved very costly for the young artillery gunners, as there were some direct hits by the enemy rockets on our artillery guns costing five American lives. Rodgers (Doc) Denny, Whitney Ferguson 111, Michael Gruenwald J., John R. Jackson, and Tommy L. Robinson were the KIAs that night.

The enemy came with their rocket and mortar attack, but just like they came they left. It was said at that time the enemy had attacked in retaliation because the two artillery batteries were blasting them day and night with harassing fires. Maybe the commie generals did not know but that's what our artillery is supposed to do and no one had to tell those young red legs what to do, they knew what to do, and they did it.

Unfortunately that night we lost some outstanding artillery men!

CHAPTER 28

The Battle of the Goose Egg

The next three or four days would be the longest days of my life. The Cav headquarters was planning a new mission for us. Our new Battalion Commander LTC Ivan Boone was right in the middle of all the planning and of course Wild Card (Charlie Company) was not far from his thoughts. The overall operation would be called The Goose Egg because it would be shaped like a giant goose egg in shape.

The perimeter of the goose egg would consist of several armor tank companies that would advance toward the middle of the so-called egg. The tanks would be augmented by armor personnel units who would also advance toward the middle. The tank units would be provided by the Big Red One (1st Infantry Division) while the personnel carriers and the infantry on board would be provided by our own 11th Armored Cavalry.

There would be an Airmobile Company dropped in the middle of the goose egg to be used as an intelligent gatherer and if needed act as a blocking force. For this assignment Wild Card was selected and we started our preparations. We were told to take lots of ammo, way past the basic load and lots of grenades both explosive and in colors to signal our location. We loaded up after Capt. Brittintham gave the preparatory command. Lt. Kopec and I wondered why so much ammo if our main mission was intelligence gathering. Rumors were that there was an enemy Regiment located west of La Kai in the triple canopy jungles. Sniffer reports and enemy sightings in the area indicated a large concentration of enemy in the area nearby.

The day arrived and we gathered at the pickup zone outside LZ Grant. In sorties of six helicopters carrying a platoon at a time we airlifted, of course we were first, but I was not too concerned as my platoon had executed about fifty of the landings and I knew that they were ready. That morning my count from SFC Albert Rodriguez was a total of thirty three including ourselves. The second platoon would be picked up after we were dropped off, and the third platoon plus the motor platoon would follow. Capt. Brittingham would be with the second platoon along with his Radio operators and his Artillery FO Lt. Joel Snyder.

The airlift for my platoon was accompanied by the Air Rocket Artillery (ARA) which were two heavily equip Cobras and two LOH's or Light Observation Helicopters which were also armed with a mini-guns and a grenade chunkers. I felt comfortable with our escort and like I said my men and I had gone on many of these ventures. Every one of them was sitting near the door, like myself with our feet dangling and ready to jump. The machine gunners on each side of the Huey were always ready to engage the enemy. My only concern was that it would be about a thirty minute turn around time for the Hueys to bring the next platoon to our location.

As we neared the landing area I could see very heavy jungle below us, made up of triple canopy mahogany threes and the ever present jungle vines. I could see the monkeys flying from tree to tree. To me the monkeys were telling us not to land, to keep on going. The ARA and the Artillery units back at LZ Grant opened up with their prep of the area. They dropped many HE (high explosive)) rounds and many white prosperous rounds. The landing zone was an inferno and as the artillery slacked off the Cobra gun ships opened up with their prep of the possible enemy hiding places followed by the little LOH's spraying the area with the mini guns and the grenade chunkers.

To my surprise there was no enemy movement nor return fire and my men and I jumped to the ground and ran for cover, and the Hueys took of to bring the next group of soldiers to our location. The Hueys arrived with the second load which was the second platoon and I moved mine further away from the landing zone and into cover and concealment.

The flying machines made their third trip bringing Lt. Shultz with his third platoon and again I moved my soldiers deeper into the jungle. Finally the mortar platoon arrived and we were all together.

Lt. Victor M. Villarreal having a chat with Lt.
Shultz before the big confrontation.

Capt Brittingham radioed me to look for a good place to camp and plan out our strategies and I did. As I looked for a good camp ground I noticed a lot of the area had been previously used by other units and I wondered if it had been friends or foes. I noticed some of the trees had been cut with saws and quickly assume that it was foes that had cut them for use in building underground bunkers. I informed my commander that I suspected we were near an enemy headquarters or hospital because of the cut trees.

We quickly made a perimeter that we could defend. We put out listing posts and set claymore's to be able to defend our position. The commander called for a quick meeting of the platoon leaders and platoon sergeants. We established communication with the surrounding landing zones for artillery support and gave them our location and set up firing points for the different batteries. We had only gone several hundred yards from the original landing zone and although we have not received enemy fire we were ready to defend our positions.

Dark started to set in and if there was any enemy out there we would soon know. The commander sent out Sharky (SGT Rex Gordon) and his men to do some night probing. Sharky's men detected a lot of moment that night but no contact was made with the enemy. At the main perimeter we all so experienced a lot of noise coming from enemy movement, again no contact was made with them. Morning crept up on us with a heavy fog and we set out to meet with the commander again. Capt. Brittingham advised us that some of the tank and armor units had made light but steady contact with the enemy all night long. There had been no major confrontation with the enemy units.

The plan for the day was that I would take my platoon on a search and destroy operation. The rest of the company would remain in place waiting the outcome of my operation. I advised Sgt. Rodriguez that we would be traveling light but with all our ammunition. Sgt. John Perkins readied his two machine-gun squads with all their ammo. I advised my platoon that we would be going into what we thought was a heavy concentration of enemy forces. I could see in their faces that they were ready. My new radio operator SGT. John Nurse and FO Alvin Burke did maintenance on their radios and made sure that they were charged up and ready for a long trip.

I advised my point man Kenny Covington to proceed in a northwesterly direction being very careful where he took us. This was a command that was not necessary with Kenny. This young man was ready at all times to take on all comers. He was probably one of the youngest men in my platoon but this young man you could bet your life on. He was a natural born outdoorsman and he knew how to live and stay alive and hostile environment.

As Kenny moved out into the jungle he was backed up by an and M-79 man and another rifleman then I was behind that rifleman and then there was SGT. John Nurse my radio man and Alvin Burke. Sgt. John Perkins was in front of the first machine-gun crew with his trusty shotgun. Behind Perkins was an M-60 machine gun crew with California Don on the trigger and I mean on the trigger. Don would never hesitate to lay down a solid base of fire from his M-60 machine-gun. It was a known fact that as soon as bullets started flying California Don would charge forward with his M-60 firing a rapid barrage of lead and giving the rest of us time to reach some cover.

Behind California Don were his four ammo bearers one being a huge man known as Water Buffalo for his huge size loaded and ready for action. They were followed by several riflemen and M 79 men. Another M-60 machine gun (Malone) and his crew followed ready to respond to any situation. Toward the end of the platoon were more rifleman and SFC Rodriguez. As they filed past me and into the jungle I could see the look in their faces and they were ready to do their job. David Heiner, John Howell, John Bailey, Don Sheriff, (Hoss) Parrish, and the rest of the men which by now total 33 including my small staff of RTOs and SGT Perkins and SFC Rodriquez.

We traveled most of the morning without incident but about noon Kenny Covington came upon an opening in the jungle that was still covered by the triple canopy jungle but it was open where we could walk around and we found seven Army (enemy) type trucks. These trucks were empty and abandoned with nothing visible. They were fairly new but of very old body styles. They seemed to have been abandoned by someone in an awful hurry or perhaps they were left there to be used in later date to transport what ever needed to be moved.

I called Capt. Brittingham and advised him of the find. His instructions were to destroy them and with great pleasure we did. In a matter of minutes the seven new trucks were blown up and in flames. We felt that we had accomplished our mission and there was no fresh sign of the enemy so I elected to return to the main perimeter. We traveled back using a different route.

As we traveled back we noticed more enemy sign as if large numbers of troops had moved through the area. The jungle was thick and although it had been opened by the B-52 bombs somewhat, was still like a big green wall. Some of the bomb craters that had been made by the bombs were so large that clear water had already formed at the bottom.

Schwabe and Lt. Villarreal in triple canopy jungle near LZ Grant.

As we traveled and worked our way around the bomb craters we continued to see heavy signs of enemy activity that was everywhere. At one point in our travels Kenny Covington advised me that he could hear enemy coming toward us. And a quick reactionary move I advised my men to get into one of the bomb craters since this was the only cover available.

I sent the men into the bomb crater and went with John Nurse and Alvin Burke to get some cover behind some mahogany trees. Within a few minutes the lead element of the enemy was visible. They kept moving as if to parallel us completely unaware that we were so close. Before long more enemy appeared and the command element was now in front of us. I signaled to my men to get ready which was a command that was not necessary because as I turned to look at them they were ready.

As I looked at the enemy column I knew we were outnumbered but there was no way of walking away from this. I had to engage and hope for the best. As I looked at the enemy my heart was thumping very fast and I knew that this was one of the biggest challenges I had faced so far in the war. Many thoughts came to my head of what would happen to me and all my men, but I knew that they were very good soldiers and that when they were in a fight they were ready to fight. Still I wondered what other platoon leaders and commanders had done when faced with the same situation.

I slid into a bomb crater and Hoss Parrish is pulling me out.

I didn't have to wonder very long because as I looked at the enemy column they stopped moving forward. They had either seen something they did not like or felt the presence of my platoon. I raised my Car-15 in the direction of their commander and his staff and radio operators. I made one last look out of the corner of my eye to the right toward my men and all I saw was that everybody was poised and ready waiting for the signal. I pulled the trigger and the automatic burst out of my little rifle was just the beginning of a loud roar that came from other platoon members all firing as rapid as they could their rifles and machine guns and grenade launchers as I loaded another magazine I could see them doing the same and it was just one continuous burst of fire. The enemy unit was right in the middle of our kill zone.

I wondered how long I could keep this rate of fire without running out of ammunition and becoming the victim of our enemy. I could see that there were many enemy soldiers down and many yelling in pain from their wounds so I turned to my radio operator to locate some air strikes that might be in my area. As SGT. John Nurse scrambled the air to locate the air support we needed. I advised Sgt Alvin Burke to get the artillery ready. John quickly made contact with the forward air controller in the area and he advised me that he was on his way and within a few minutes he would be in our area. He advised me that he had a sortie of bombers within minutes notice but he also asked me to mark my position.

I popped a yellow smoke to mark my position and gave him directions to the enemy positions. He quickly responded that we were too close to the enemy and it was unsafe to bomb. I had a decision to make and I quickly made it. I pulled out a purple smoke grenade and tossed in as far as I could behind us. I advised the FAC to reevaluate my position quickly as I feared for a counterattack from the enemy. He flew by and advised me that we were the safe distance for his jets to bomb and they were on the way.

The bombers were on the way and I was proud and happy to see that everyone of my men was still safe and fighting. I could see that what was left of the enemy were regrouping and getting ready to attack. One of the greatest feelings that American in combat can have is to see our Air Force jets in action. It seems like there's a split second where they are suspended in the air as they dived in on their targets.

All of a sudden the jets were upon us dropping their 500 pound bombs and the loudest explosions were witnessed. At the time of the explosions it seemed that I had been lifted and slammed into the ground. I quickly looked at my men to see if they were safe. They were a little bit confused and full of powdered earth created by the bombs and I could not hear what they were saying. I just kept hearing a loud buzzing in my ears. There appeared to be no casualties and for that I was grateful.

All of sudden California Don threw down his M-60 and started yelling. I ran over to him and embraced him because I noticed a wild look in his eyes. Suddenly it seemed like his tongue was protruding more than normally out of his mouth. He was a big strong kid and I was having a rough time keeping him down so Bailey and Heiner came over to help me hold him down. It seemed as if he wanted to take the enemy on hand to hand combat situation.

I evaluated the situation. I could not see the enemy moving around and I assume that the jets had taken care of most of them and it was time to move. We were not receiving incoming gunfire nor were rockets blasting us. So we quickly moved and we picked up our equipment and our only casualty and headed toward base camp. The FAC could not detect any movement among the enemy. I thanked the jets for their help, meanwhile the ARA helicopters started to make passes blasting with their rocket and mini-guns firing while we slipped into the jungle and back to our perimeter.

That had been very close. To engage a large enemy force and to come out with only one casualty was a very good feeling. I could see my platoon members were feeling very good and we got back to the company area called in for a med-vac and sent California Don for medical attention. We never saw California Don again nor heard or saw a medical report on him so we assumed that he was sent home.

I reported to Capt. Brittingham and he was very pleased with the overall outcome of the contact. I advised him that I didn't know if we had been followed but I felt pretty sure that most of the enemy soldiers were dead or very seriously wounded. The commander said that in our absence they had been receiving continuous mortar fire and it was going to be in our best interest to move. He asked me to take the lead and look for a good perimeter for the evening where we could dig in and defend our positions.

I gathered my men because I knew they were tired and explained to them what our new mission was. We headed in a new direction and traveled for several hundred yards or meters and I started to look for a new campground. Soon I noticed that there were a lot of large trees cut down and this indicated heavy bunkers ahead or even an enemy hospital in the area. I could see that even large trees have been cut down and removed so I knew we were getting close to an enemy headquarters or medical facility. It would be useless to go further because darkness would be upon us soon.

I mounted one of the stumps and started to direct my men into a defensive position. Then all of a sudden I heard that voice again in perfect Spanish telling me to get off the stump quickly. I jumped to one side when a long machine-gun burst hit the stump. It appeared that I was the target of an enemy soldier with an automatic weapon most probably mounted on a tree. My men reacted by opening fire in every direction they could see a possible target. For the next two minutes we had a battle on our hands. I had not been hit miraculously thanks to that mysterious voice that gave me the warning. I didn't have time to think who or what it was but I had heard it before back in the Michelin.

I advised the commander that I was in contact with the enemy and that I would direct the rest of the company as best I could into defensive positions where they could begin digging in. It seemed that my men were scoring hits on the snipers because soon the small arms fires were silenced. Then came an occasional mortar round as serving more of a harassing fire. I instructed my men to begin digging in as second and third platoons were already in their positions and beginning to dig in. In my opinion we were in for a long night of fighting.

I met again with Capt. Brittingham and advised him that all the troops were in place and had started to dig in. He advised me that he was sending Sharky and his men in the direction that I had received the fire earlier. Sharky and his men departed very cautiously into the jungle. It was not very long after that that they started to receive small arms fire. Darkness crept in but now we had better foxholes and were ready for the night. That night I felt afraid, afraid that our company would be overrun and we would all be killed.

That night proved to be a very long one since Sharky and his men were under fire most of the night. We could hear enemy movement to the front of our positions and in the direction that Sharky had taken. There were moments when we could hear Sharky and his men heavily engaged in combat with the enemy. There was an occasional yell from our men or from the enemy and again a lot of movement from the enemy in our front.

The commander advised us on the radio that he wanted to pull Sharky out but darkness and the heavy contact with the enemy made it impossible. Sharky radioed in that one of his men, James O'Shaughnessy was seriously wounded. His remaining men and himself were okay so far but running low on ammunition. Our company FO Lt. Joel Snyder directed the 105 and 155 batteries at the enemy positions. He kept the barrage going for most of the night. Judging from the yells of the enemy we knew that he was trying to keep his call sign of Birth Control 6 alive and well.

Lt. Joel Snyder and his radio operators were busy directing the shells upon the enemy who in most likelihood were in heavy bunkers. If there were any enemy not in bunkers he made them pay dearly for it. Sgt. Alvin Burt my artillery FO also helped Snyder and the other forward observers direct rounds upon the NVA. And all night long the artillery kept the blasting. To me the artillery rounds didn't sound that loud anymore not since the air strike. Little did I know that I had lost my hearing forever.

Lt. Joel Snyder FO (Birth Control 6) loading a 155 Howitzer at LZ Grant.

Finally, in the morning Lt. Kopec and the Second Platoon were able to pull Sharky and his men out of harms way. Sharky looked much older than the day before and his men were a bit shaken from fighting all night in very close quarters and James O'Shaughnessy was dead. Yes, the youngster that was always in good spirits always willing to make a friend had died during the night. When the word spread of Jim's death you could see that the men were saddened. Here was a good All-American boy who had come to Vietnam to do his duty without asking questions just follow orders and now he was gone.

Now we were all together but it seemed that the small arms fire had ceased and the mortar rounds would come it only occasionally. Perhaps the enemy had retreated, or had gone deeper into their bunker complex. Maybe they were regrouping to assault our positions in force? What ever they were planning or doing we would find out soon. After a breakfast of cold rations we cleaned and checked our weapons. We were ready for another day in the bush.

Lt. Victor M. Villarreal having a cold lunch of C-Rations
with a large bottle of tabasco hot sauce nearby.

I always wondered what kept these fighting men going. They had fought all day yesterday and had been on alert all night long. I really don't think that any of them had gotten any serious rest or sleep. Yet, here they were ready to go at it again. I think back and wonder what it is, that an American fighting man is made of.

Capt. Brittingham gave us the mission for the day. Third Platoon led by Lt. Schultz would move forward through my position and the direction where Sharky had met resistance the night before and make a wedge and we would follow. In case of any enemy resistance first platoon under my direction would move forward and assist the third platoon. Second Platoon led by Lt Kopec would protect the 4th Platoon (mortar platoon) and the HHC. Capt. Brittingham, Lt. Snyder and all NCO' and RTOs of the HHC would remain with Lt. Kopec.

As Lt. Schultz neared my position he smiled and said "I'd rather be home than where I'm going". Schultz was a very nice man. He was much older than the other lieutenants but it made us feel good because he always had good advice and comments for us. He had been in the National Guard and was activated for the Vietnam War and that's why he was older than us. We had a few laughs, then he darted into the jungle with his men.

Schultz had gone several hundred meters into the jungle when hell broke loose. His men were engaged in combat with a very large enemy force. He was under automatic small arms fire, mortar and rocket attack. He had been returning fire as best they could. Suddenly he radioed in that he was under heavy attack from a large NVA force. Lt. Snyder started pounding away with his artillery units and it sounded like an inferno.

The commander radioed me and gave me the order to get ready to assist the 3rd Platoon. I instructed my men to get ready and get all ammunition and light backpacks ready to move. I loaded up my usual 37 magazines for my Car-15 and I checked on my sidearm for which I had only had six rounds. I had my 45 pistol wrapped in a oiled hand towel. I had not used my pistol since the day of the water buffalo.

With Kenny Covington leading the away we proceeded in the direction that the third platoon had taken. We proceeded several hundred meters then we started to see the action. While the shooting was going on at all times we had not seen any of our men. I started to spread the men so that we could not miss anyone of the wounded. We were receiving mortar fire from an undisclosed location.

The automatic weapons continue to harass us as did the snipers. We could hear the snap crackle and pop from the AK-47s coming at us. Once you hear an AK-47 being fired at you, you will always remember that awful sound. My men and I started to engage the enemy. All of a sudden we were in for a free for all.

My men and I were engaging snipers and even automatic weapons mounted on trees. The mortars continued to come in as if nothing could stop him. I was unable to direct artillery fire because I did not know where the third platoon men were exactly. We continued in that direction we had seen Lt. Schultz travel and soon we began to find wounded soldiers. There seem to be many wounded soldiers on a path leading away from our campground. I instructed my men to start carrying them back to our base camp. I also told them to come back so we could find the rest. After perhaps 30 minutes of intense contact with the enemy we found Lt. Schulz and some more men. I surrounded him with my men while continuing to fight the enemy in the bunkers and in the trees. Lt. Schulz was wounded and unable to move. His radio operator and platoon medic were very seriously wounded.

We looked around and found the remaining members of the third platoon who were still able to fight returning fire to the enemy. These men were showing some grit because they were facing a large element to their front. The rest of the platoon were laying all around Lt. Schulz's position wounded. The firing was pretty intense there for several minutes. Finally my men and I and what remained of the third platoon were able to suppress most of the small arms fire. The mortars continue to harass us.

I instructed my men to pick up all the wounded and take them back to our perimeter. By this time the contact with the enemy had been so fierce that I personally was out of ammunition. We picked up Lt. Schulz and his men and also my wounded soldiers that had been hit during the fighting. We started back toward the base camp with what we thought was everyone. I personally picked up the wounded radio operator who had been shot in one eye. I carried him all the way back to the camp. Somehow, even as exhausted as everyone was we made it to the perimeter. Capt. Brittingham was there to greet us. He had picked up shrapnel wound from the incoming mortars.

I informed the Captain of what I had seen and what we had done in order to retrieve the third platoon. There were many wounded, but so far no fatalities. Lt. Schulz would be unable to remain in a combat zone as were many of his soldiers and even some of mine. My medic took complete charge of the wounded. I made a headcount and there was one soldier missing from the third platoon. It was the medic, somehow he had been left behind. I remember that I had seen him next to the radio operator that I personally brought back myself. I also remembered that he was still alive even though he was badly wounded.

I looked at my men and I could see their exhausted look. Those that were not wounded were covered with blood and debris from the fierce fighting we had just encountered. I wondered who I could send back for the missing soldier and face what we had faced earlier. I knew I couldn't do it, they had risked it all and were exhausted or wounded. I picked up a 30 round clip for my car-15 and loaded it, placed it in my rifle and summoned Sgt. Rodriguez and Sgt. Perkins. I left them in charge of my men and asked them to begin placing them back into their foxholes. I told them I was going back for the missing soldier. They both gave me a hard stare but they knew they could not change my mind.

I dashed back into the combat zone but somehow I ended taking a different route. I started to look for the missing soldier or the place where I had last seen him. Suddenly I came upon an open area and there in front of my eyes was a mortar position with five enemy soldiers putting rounds into it. So this was one of the mortars that had been harassing us all day. They were so busy with their fire mission that they could not see me a short distance from them.

I aimed my Car-15 at the mortar crew and fired at them on automatic. I could see all five enemy soldiers go down. I walked over to them and they appear to be all dead. That was good I thought because that's all the ammunition I had. I continued looking for the wounded soldier until I found him. He was very seriously wounded. One of his shoulders was almost completely torn off and he lost a lot of blood. I assumed he had been hit by a B-40 rocket. When he saw me he managed a smile and that's all I needed, I regained my energies and managed to pick him up.

I picked him up by putting his left arm around my neck on the left side and by him grabbing my left shoulder. With my right shoulder I wrapped him by the waist placing my right hand on his belt and grabbing it as tight as I could. And with my rifle slung after all it was empty, I started to head back toward the our company perimeter base camp. The soldier was very big and heavy. With the blood and grime running down his back and toward my hand where I had him by the belt, it was very hard for me to control him. There was some small arms fire coming but the mortars were silent for now. It made my movement somewhat easier. I could think of nothing else but getting back to our base camp.

In route I came right back to the mortar position. As I got closer to bypass it one of the enemy soldiers started to move. There was not very much I could do about it since I was out of ammo so I continued to move past this position. I went maybe thirty meters when I tripped over a jungle vine and went down with my wounded soldier. As I started to get up I noticed that one of the soldiers from the mortar position had stood up and was pointing a B-40 rocket launcher at me. I picked up the soldier and continued to walk away when there was a loud explosion and as a rocket hit the tree next to me. I felt a sting on left arm around the elbow and another sting on my back. I realized this little guy was trying to kill us.

I placed the soldier on the ground and in wondering what to do I remembered my sidearm. I reached for my holster and pulled out my 45 pistol wrapped in that oily dirty green towel I had wrapped on it. I pointed it at the soldier who was standing there looking at me and probably wondering how I had survived the rocket blast. I've pulled the trigger and nothing happened. Then I remembered that I never carried a round in the chamber, and quickly pulled the receiver back and placed one in. I headed straight toward the enemy soldier pulling the trigger as I went, and by the time it clicked empty he was down. I don't know whether I hit him once or six times, it just doesn't matter, he went down. Killing a young soldier did not give any special pleasure, but after all he was trying hard to kill us.

I picked up my man and proceeded back to the camp without incident. I reported to the Commander that I had retrieved the last man and that all our troops had been extracted from the ambush site. When I returned to my platoon everyone was happy, we had some wounded but no one was dead. But I could see by the tired faces that this could not continue very long. We were advised that there would be no more med-a-vacs dust-offs that day. Capt Brittingham advised me that he was taking the last helicopter with wounded soldiers into LZ Grant to get treated for his wound. (Several months later I was awarded the Silver Star for that day).

I felt somewhat let down, because now without the Capt. and with the exception of Lt. Kopec, and Lt. Snyder, I was alone. I knew that there would be more fighting and the men were in no shape to continue fighting. I requested heavy artillery strikes on the last location I had the enemy pin pointed. I asked the battalion operations officer to continue the air support and if possible a B-52 strike. There was no doubt that we had stumbled into the enemy regiment we were looking for. I also knew that we were heavily outnumbered and that the NVA would like nothing better that to wipe us out.

If they could take on our armor units and mounted personnel carriers they were willing to stand their ground. I felt that to continue fighting these units would come at a very costly price in human life. The third platoon was very weak having lost their command element and many of their men. My first platoon was also missing some of the men that had been wounded in the retrieving of the third platoon. The second platoon was for the most part in-tack and under the leadership of Lt. Kopec would be our strongest element. The mortar platoon had some losses but I couldn't use them too much to attack the enemy. The best solution would be to be extracted and have the enemy bombed by our B-52s.

I asked Lt. Kopec to move us to a new location where we could set up for the night and get ready to fight what I felt was a counter offensive coming from the enemy. I knew that the counter offensive the enemy would mount would be fierce. The enemy knew that if they kept close to us, it would minimize the artillery strikes and deny us the use of B-52s against them. The second platoon moved in a direction away from the enemy contact that we had established. Lt. Kopec had picked a good location heavily wooded yet it had some open areas between us and the enemy force. These open areas would serve as killing zones if the enemy decided to mass an attack. I instructed Lt. Joel Snyder (FO) to place some marking rounds where we could drop artillery in a hurry in case of a counteroffensive was mounted by the North Vietnamese Army (NVA) Regulars. For the past two days we had been facing nothing but regular communist troops and they were well trained.

We settled in for the night feeling somewhat secure that we could make a stand if we had to. That night Sgt Nurse my RTO and Sgt Burke and I sat down to have a meal of cold C-Rations. I opened a can of *jalapenos* stuffed with tuna to spice up the meal. As John Nurse bit into one of the peppers he said that his adopted Hispanic family back in Gary Indiana was going to be so proud of him eating peppers. He went on to say that he had not been able to eat them before and his adopted mother a lady named Mae Costa had always encouraged him to eat them, but they were too hot for him. He said she was going to be surprised and proud of him. To me it was no great ceremony to eat a jalapeno, since I had eaten them since childhood.

The enemy made several probes of our position but Lt. Snyder and his RTOs quickly engaged them with the artillery fires. All went well with one minor incident when an artillery round fell short and landed in our perimeter hitting Malone one of my M-60 gunners in the arm. In the morning we sent for a med-a-vac and sent him for treatment.

I advised Lt. Kopec to move us in a direction toward LZ Grant even though we were about ten clicks away. He started to move and quickly came under heavy fire from his front. We were pinned down and unable to make forward progress. All of a sudden a Huey could be heard circling over us but very high. It was Roving Gambler 6 (LTC Ivan Boone) wanting to know what was wrong. I advised him we were under fire, and that our lead element was not making progress because of the intense small arms fire.

He came over the radio and instructed me to have my men fix bayonets and rout the enemy from their positions. I didn't know if this man had missed out on the fact that we were outnumbered and had suffered many casualties the previous days. I did not want to lose any more men than what we had lost already. I responded that I did not know how to rout the enemy with a bayonet in heavy jungle terrain. I asked him to come down and show me how to do it. He responded by saying that if I did not know how he would relieve me and get someone that knew how. At that time the Huey disappeared and he left us alone.

Lt. Kopec continued hammering away at the enemy and Lt. Snyder kept on blasting away with his batteries of artillery. Those redlegs at LZ Grant were not abandoning us. Within a few minutes two LOHs appeared on the scene. A cherry voice came over the radio and said, "This is Silver 1-1 and Silver 1-2 at your service, what can we do for you". At first I thought I was hearing things. Here were two small gun ships when we needed them most. But most of all the voice on the radio sounded like the voice of my friend and former roommate Lt. Kenny Dies of Beaumont, Texas.

The first thing that came to me was "Kenny is that you". I had not heard from him since he left for flight school. He came over the radio and said "Vic, this is your old roommate, can we help you out." "You sure can" I replied, we have not been able to move as we are pinned down pretty good". "We will open some lanes for you to move" he replied. And both of the LOHs went to work on the enemy with their mini-guns and grenade launchers.

In a few minutes Lt. Kopec was beginning to move. The LOHs were running short on ammo when Kenny came over the radio and said that they were going to La Kai to reload. I thanked him and his partner when he flew over our position and three shots were heard. He flew over one more time and two more shots were heard. I asked what was wrong and he said "Nothing I was shooting at the *gooks* with my side arm (pistol), but now I am out of ammo. I could not leave my old buddy knowing I still had rounds in my revolver" he added and left.

Yes Sir, that was Kenny Dies, what a gutsy character! Was this chivalry or what?

After the LOHs left we were able to continue moving as Lt. Kopec's second platoon moved forward but fighting all the way. Lt. Snyder continued to blast the enemy with the 105 and 155 batteries he was directing. We were able to move about a click when we sat down for the night. Again we dug in for the night and I requested to be extracted from the area as I felt that with the remaining men we had we would not be able to put up a big fight against the large concentration of enemy troops.

To my surprise Major Billy Brown the Operations Officer radioed me that we would be pulled out the next day if we could get to an extraction site some eight hundred meters away. I devised the plan for the next day. Lt. Kopec would continue to led us out of the area and in the direction of the extraction LZ. Lt. Snyder would continue blasting the enemy in every direction with the artillery as we moved. My 1st platoon would bring up the rear reinforced by the remainder of the 3rd Platoon and the Mortar Platoon.

We would act as a blocking force if the enemy realized we were headed for an extraction point and wanted to rush us from the rear. I divided the men into groups of three who would stay back and shoot anyone following us, then they would rejoin the unit and another group would fall back, etc. That worked real well and the riflemen were able to pick off many enemy soldiers who were rushing to stay close to us and avoid the artillery rounds. You could see the gusto some of the men like Parrish, Heiner, Sherrif, Howe, Schuabe and John Bailey were taking in mowing the enemy down. It was like a turkey shoot and my men had the upper hand.

Lt. Kopec continued to fight the elements in our front and we kept the unit moving. Soon Kopec reached the extraction point and I called for the Hueys to pick him up, followed by the 3rd Platoon and Mortars Platoon. The last set of Hueys picked up my platoon and a few stragglers and we were all extracted (It seemed like a long time that we waited for those Hueys, but they came). As we lifted over the trees the door gunners opened up and some of my men joined them. Within minutes we were at LZ Grant and getting off the choppers.

Capt Brittingham was there to greet us with one arm bandaged up. He reached over to shake my hand and said "Thanks Vic, for taking care of my men." I quickly replied "They are my men now Captain." At that we both laughed and entered LZ Grant. LTC Boone did not come to greet us and I never heard about being insubordinate again.

Sometimes I wonder if the North Vietnamese General commanding the NVA Regiment knew what he had run into. If he only knew that it was three twenty one year old spunky lieutenants (Kopec, Snyder and Villarreal) and a group of very determined soldiers, some of them not old enough to shave yet.

CHAPTER 29

The John Nurse and David Heiner Story

The return to LZ Grant meant rebuilding Charlie Company. We were down to about half of the original number of soldiers from the day we had left into the jungle. Some of the men had light wounds and would re-cooperate at our stand down at Grant. Some of the men were more seriously wounded and some would not return to combat at all. I continued in command of the company during the rebuilding. Orders had been cut on me as commander and Capt. Brittingham stayed around the TOC for the most part.

Every day we could see FNGs (F-------New Guys) reporting to the Battalion Sergeant Major and after a short briefing they would report to me. This went on for several weeks and I would assign the new men to the experienced soldiers on the defense bunkers. At night we were short of men and some of the supply clerks an cooks would fill in for perimeter guard. They all understood that the defense of LZ Grant was a job for everyone since our lives depended on it.

The landing zone had been hit three times and we could expect another attack at any time. One thing for sure we could not afford any more human losses. Even the artillery red legs (gunners) were wide alert for any sign of enemy. They had some close calls also and lost some men. I felt real good working side by side with the artillery men, it seemed to me whoever was assigning the men to the guns was being very particular about his selections. I felt that if the enemy attacked he would be in for a surprise because even though we were weak in numbers we now had lots of experience.

One day I was conversing with SFC Albert Rodriguez the Platoon Sergeant and SSG John Perkins the Crew Served Weapons NCO and my RTO Sgt. John Nurse about our situation. All of a sudden John Nurse asked me if I could find a rear job for him because he was a bit shaken with what had happened while we were in the jungle. I could see that John was feeling the stress from too much close combat. His situation was easy to understand, we had been at close combat for several days and it was enough to shake anyone.

The rear jobs available for an infantryman were not many. Either he was assigned to the field mess or the perimeter cleanup detail. The mess hall details were not many and the cleanup detail was not the best since it involved burning the human feces in cut off drums by stirring them with diesel and setting it on fire and occasionally stirring the drum to make sure it all burned. Personally I would rather face the NVA. Neither job was suited for Sgt. John Nurse after the action he had just participated in.

John Bailey and John Nurse at LZ Grant shortly before the accident.

I realized I had a situation on hand, John Nurse was suffering from battle fatigue. I had to do something for him yet I had to be fair to the rest of the men. John continued talking about how he felt and then he opened up even more. I also had in my mind that I had left Walter Hoxworth behind at the base camp the last time we had being at Grant protecting the perimeter. Walter's death was always on my mind, if I had only taken him with us.

"You have been a very good platoon leader 1-6," he said.

"Well John, you have done a very good job on the radio since we lost Harold Hopper to the snake bite," I responded.

"You took good care of us these last few days," he went on getting sentimental.

"John all I did was do what I thought could save as many of the men as possible," I went on.

"I don't know if you know but the men are writing you up for the Medal of Honor for retrieving that wounded soldier by yourself," he went on. He pointed toward SFC Rodriguez and SSG Perkins who were nodding in concurrence.

"John, I'm going to repeat a phrase that I have not said in years, *I no hero*, I'm just a soldier who came to Viet-Nam to do the best I could and that's all."

John laughed "Yeah, 1-6, you are speaking in broken English and with an accent," he replied.

"Look here John, if your going to sit there and make fun of my English I am going to send you before a firing squad ," I joked.

We all started to laugh at my last remark. "John, go to the perimeter and look for Dave Heiner and both of you report to the NCO that is working on the claymores and pu gas drums in the concertina wire near the water point," I instructed John Nurse. John left to look for Heiner and I sat there with the two NCOs, Rodriguez and Perkins thinking of what to do about John. I sent SFC Rodriguez to look for the 1st Sergeant to see where we might be able to place him.

It seemed like a few minutes when a loud explosion was heard coming from the perimeter. Somehow I just knew that it was coming from the direction I had sent Nurse and Heiner. The sick feeling in my stomach told me they were in serious trouble. I ran as fast as I could to the perimeter and I saw the smoke billowing from an explosion and I could see several bodies on the concertina wire and they were on fire.

Someone threw me an army blanket which I wrapped around the

first body and started to run with him toward a med-a-vac that had just landed at Grant but it was several hundred meters away. Someone wrapped the other soldier and did the same as I. When I reached the chopper I looked at the badly charred body in the blanket and it was John Nurse and he was very seriously burned. All of a sudden he spoke and said "Am I going to make it 1-6?," I looked at him and lied "Yes, John you are going to make it". I looked over to the other side of the Huey and noticed that even though Dave Heiner was badly hurt he was not as badly burned as John.

The Med-Vac cranked up, and got ready for takeoff and I looked down and there were pieces of John Nurse's flesh on my shirt. The Huey lifted and neither of the two men came back to the unit. Several days later I was informed that John Nurse had died of his wounds and Dave Heiner was alive but badly burned and had been sent somewhere for more intensive medical attention.

I was happy for Dave but very sad for John. Several years ago I located Dave Heiner back in his hometown of Delta, Pa., where he lives with his wife and their twin boys that are already grown young men. In June 2009, Linda and I, my sister Ofelia and Irma Perales (a friend) met with David and Debbie Heiner at Union Station, Washington DC and it was quite a reunion.

David Heiner and Victor M. Villarreal meet in June of 2009 at Union Station, Washington D.C. forty years after the Viet-Nam War.

I cursed myself blaming myself for the death of John Nurse. What could I have done differently to have avoided his death. It's this damn war, no matter what you do to keep your soldiers safe the enemy situation changes and something happens to put them in danger. Many times I just stare at the ceiling thinking about the soldiers that died and what they would be today if they had lived. Soon we lost SFC Rodriguez to rotation. The quiet older man who had been my back up for over six months was leaving to an assignment at West Point. I was going to miss this man who had been there when I arrived and never backed down from any situation. The men all respected him and I was going to miss him.

We would remain at LZ Grant for a few more days until we had regained some of our strength in numbers. We were airlifted and taken some eight clicks away and dropped off. It was a cold landing and we regrouped before heading into the jungle. That night a Huey came in and dropped off Capt. Brittingham. I was curios what he was doing there so we met with my NCOs and Lt. Kopec. The Captain pulled out a bottle of *tequila* with a worm in it. He passed it around and soon the worm disintegrated and we were drinking it along with the *tequila*. Soon he got around to what he wanted to say.

He started by saying that I had been given a new assignment in the TOC as S-3 Air and he was taking over the company again. He went on to say that I had been commander for 30 days and had received credit for being the CO. He thanked me and I went to gather with my platoon and tell them that I was leaving. With SFC Rodriguez gone I named SSG Perkins as the acting platoon leader. I knew that John Perkins would do a good job because he was very cautious.

The next morning I departed on a Huey and as the chopper lifted it gave me a moment of sadness. I had spent many days and nights with these wonderful young soldiers. I also knew that as time passed on I would forget some names, but I would never forget their deeds, especially their bravery.

I reported to LZ Grant and my Battalion Commander LTC Ivan Boone. LTC Boone was older than my two previous commanders LTC James Dingeman and the late LTC Peter Gorvad. I had already formed an opinion about this man after my encounter with him in the fix bayonets incident. I knew that this man did not posses the leadership style of the two other commanders. I had never seen this man out in the field with the grunts nor walking point either, he was different.

Maybe I was being too hard on him but the truth was I did not respect him. I had to work with him until rotation and time can go very slow in a combat zone.

CHAPTER 30

The fourth attack on LZ Grant on May 12. 1969

I was now an official member of the Roving Gambler staff as the S-Air which is like an assistant to the S-3 who is the operations officer. I lived in a little shack made up of metal culverts and sandbags. This hut could stop small arms fire but not mortar or rockets. I doubt very much if they could stop a B-40 or RPG round. Yet it was home for me and I slept very comfortably on my air mattress and covered up with my poncho liner. When it rained my cover was kept dry by the metal and sandbag roof and a small drainage ditch I had made all around my hooch.

I kept my few valuables like my camera and film there. I also had a tape recorder to hear tapes from home mostly from Linda there in my little castle. It was not much but it was all I had to call home. I was but a few feet away from the defensive berm and one of the 105s artillery pieces. Every morning I would get up, clean up and go by the artillery gun to say morning to the young red legs and then mossy on to the mess hall to get coffee and breakfast. Greasy Spoons One and Greasy Spoons Two were usually both there. Both of these Mess Sergeants took a lot a joking from the troops since they had the same name (Veasly) and one was black and the other was white. It was not uncommon to hear the soldiers ask either one "Where's your brother". These men could put up some good food considering the circumstances and took the ribbing at the same time.

Charlie Company was back in the hands of Capt. Brittingham and they had returned from the boonies. My friends Rick Kopec and John Perkins were enjoying the panoramic views that only Viet-Nam could offer. Occasionally, I would see them and I was free to talk to them on the radio. My new duties kept me busy as I was always planning new air strikes to support our troops in the field. B-52 strikes had to be preplanned so that the safety of the troops was not jeopardized. B-52 strikes ran in sorties of three planes per with normally one hundred one thousand pound bombs each.

It was not uncommon for me to plan three sorties and that meant nine planes etc. All friendly units had to be at least three clicks away but the rumble of the earth when those bombs exploded was terrible and it was hard to stay on your feet. Now and then our units would stumble onto a heavy bunker complex and I would ask them to withdraw and I would order a "Daisy Cutter" which was a twenty thousand pound bomb. It would really open up the ground and destroy the bunkers, also the Hueys could land there to drop troops for the exploitation. phase.

I had a wonderful NCO who had replaced Lonnie Murdock to assist me. We got along wonderful and that made my job easier. The situation between LTC Boone and I had not gotten better but we both were trying not to make it worse.

On May 12, 1969 we would have our last visit from the NVA at LZ Grant. It would come from a Zapper Company from the west side of the perimeter or from the direction of the Black Virgin Mountain. Zappers work using the darkness and shadows created by the jungles to make their advances. They are clad normally only in green underwear and painted their bodies black to blend in. Normally by the time you heard them they were on top of you.

On the early afternoon I was checking the perimeter to see that we had good coverage, although I was not worried after all this was my old unit Charlie Company. I stopped in the middle of the west perimeter to talk to the operator of the Quad-50 Machine gun mounted on an army truck. The operator, who liked to be called by his nickname, "Zorba the Greek" was in jolly spirits as usual. I commented on his happy mood and he said he felt he was going to kill *gooks* that night. This young soldier had become a master of his trade, as he was very good handling the Quad-50 under enemy fire. I also reminded him to move his truck with the gun mounted after dark to a new position since he had been parked at the same place all day and if there were any enemy look outs they had already spotted where he was.

As I inspected the end of the bunkers to the right or toward Cambodia I clearly notice two *gooks* talking to each other near the wood line in broad daylight. I kept my eye on them and after a short conversation one that appeared to be a VC (Viet Cong) disappeared into the woods behind him while the other came toward me thru the gaps in concertina wire. Those gaps were there so that in case of enemy action our listening posts could get back into the perimeter. As he approached me I stopped him and noticed he was one of our Kit Carsons (Interpreters) and I asked him where he had been. He answered that he was out relieving himself which I knew was a lie, because there were places inside the perimeter for that. I knew this guy had been out there making a deal with the enemy. I reported him to the NCO in charge of them and went about my business.

Shortly after dark the enemy mortars started to come in. I called Capt. Brittingham and he said his company was ready for any enemy intrusion. After the mortars quieted down several hours elapsed and then there was movement on the line reported. I had already turned in to my little hut when I heard talking in Vietnamese. I put my boots on and in the dark located my weapons. All of a sudden the voices got closer and a light flare was popped. I looked toward the opening of my hooch and in the light saw two set of legs standing there. They were completely black in color and almost naked. SAPPERS!!

I reached for my Car-15 knowing that these gooks had not seen me and I could blast them at point blank range. I pointed my rifle toward the opening and they were gone, and suddenly I heard an explosion coming from the artillery tube closest to me. I suspected they had lobbed a satchel charge at the gun crew. I came out of the hooch in a flash and headed for the TOC on a run keeping as low as possible.

I was curious and went by the interpreters tent and check in on them. One interpreter was there and he was very dead and it was the one that I had seen that after noon. Poetic justice, or coincidence it did not matter anymore. I entered the TOC and advised them that there were *gooks* in the perimeter and LTC Boone was there and ordered more security for the TOC. I left to check the perimeter and went by the Medical Tent and saw that our Doctor was already working on some wounded soldiers. I continued traveling low but fast toward Lt. Kopec's assigned area to check on my friend and his men.

I could not find Kopec but one of his bunkers had been hit and I could see a black soldier that had been a machine gunner very seriously hurt by a rocket or a Bangalore torpedo. It appeared to be Roy Lyles one of Kopec's M-60 gunners and one or both his legs were blown off. He looked at me when a flare went up and he asked me to shoot him. He said he did not want to live like that. I sat there trying to comfort him knowing full well that I would never even think of shooting him.

I got a medic to look at him and transfer him to the Medical Tent. I continued my travels and as I was getting closer to the Quad-50 truck, Zorba the Greek opened up with his deadly barrage of fire. It was the deadly fire from the Quad-and the artillery firing almost point blank that destroyed the enemy advance. Now it was going hooch by hooch shooting the Sappers that were already inside the compound. If my memory still holds, there were 47 dead Sappers and one alive and he was captured. The live Sapper admitted that they had been up in the trees surrounding Grant eating rice and drinking a little water for days before they attacked.

I finally located Lt. Kopec who was safe and sound but probably much older because of the experience. Several of his men were hurt especially Roy Lyles who ended up losing a foot and a lot of blood. There were two American soldiers dead and they were Curtis Levine Hardin and William Edward Jerse.

The Artillery Units had not fared two well after all it was obvious that they were the main target of the Sappers. A Battery 1/30 Artillery had one KIA who was Tommy L. Robinson. C Battery 1/77th Artillery had eight KIAs who were Don L. Atkins, Charles L. Barbiere, Timothy C. Donavan, John W. Drane, James L. Jordan, Robert G. Krell, Marvin E. Park and David E. Clime.

Nine dead Americans was a price too high to pay especially since we had only accounted for 47 enemy dead and one captured. The odds were too high in their favor but remember they were inside the perimeter before we knew it. Sappers are very highly trained soldiers with one mission in their mind which is to kill and destroy.

I will always remember that deadly night at LZ Grant which would be the last attack on the firebase for the TET Offensive of 1969.

CHAPTER 31

Duty at Camp Gorvad

After serving a few weeks at LZ White we were flown to do palace guard at the big palace—Phouc Vinh which had been renamed Camp Gorvad in honor of our late Battalion Commander LTC Peter Gorvad. Duty here was kind of boring as our patrols were doing clover leaf operations all around the city but I was still assigned to the Operations Office at Battalion HQ. Every day I did my air planning for air strikes wherever our units were meeting resistance and needed air strikes especially B-52 strikes.

We had received a new S-3 when we were at LZ White by the name of Robert O'Keefe, however I did not know too much about him. He seemed to have a fiery temper and it was not long after that that we started butting heads. Major Billy Brown was the peace maker between Major O'Keefe and I. LTC Boone avoided talking to me for the most part.

During the operations meetings I presented my air report and did not participate in the rest of the briefings since these men did whatever they wanted anyway. For the most part they gave me the requirements for the next day, whether it was in air strikes or air movements and with my NCO, I prepared the requirements and called them into my Air Force counterparts and then advised Major O'Keefe they were ready for the next day.

Some days were spent assigning groups of men to help out in the defoliant (Agent Orange) details. Camp Gorvad was a site that was daily being contaminated with the deadly defoliant to help in the eradication of the huge jungles around the base. You could fly around the base and for miles see nothing but dry or drying jungles that had been sprayed by the defoliant. Our units were walking on contaminated ground day in day out.

One day I was talking to WO Ralph Cline and WO Jerrold Pearlstein who were the two pilots that were flying the command Huey for us every day and I had become quite chummy with both. All of a sudden Major O'Keefe came by and said he needed the Huey to fly over A Company that was in contact with the enemy. I quickly advised him in front of Major Brown that A Company had ordered heavy artillery coverage all around their perimeter.

The pilots scrambled the Huey and I reminded WO Clime about the artillery fire mission. He looked at me and smiled, "Nothing can hurt me today baby, I am short ". The Huey lifted with the four crew members and Major O'Keefe in the direction of A Company. I resumed my S-3 functions as LTC Boone and Major Brown monitored the combat situation of A Company. In the back ground I could hear the pilots talking to the artillery as they went in to pick up Capt James Daniel the Commander of A Company so he could see the combat area from above.

All of a sudden there was silence as there was no more communication with the Huey. Yes, the Huey had been hit by a round of either friendly artillery or a rocket from the enemy. Major Robert O'Keefe, Capt. James Daniel, WO Ralph Clime, WO Jerrold Pearlstein and the two door gunners SGT Henry Mathews and SGT Raymond Voss were all dead! Yes, all dead. All of a sudden LTC Boone needed another Huey to go to the scene and asses the situation. I was not there but have been told that when LTC Boone landed and saw the conditions of the bodies he had a medical breakdown, which is somewhat understandable. Bodies that have been in aircraft crashes are not the best to observe or try to identify.

When LTC Boone returned to the TOC at Camp Gorvad he was very upset at the loss of the six men. He had been through a bad situation and was having problems coping with it. I was talking to Major Brown when he approached me and in an angry tone of voice asked me if I had advised the pilots about the fire mission. Major Brown answered for me since he had been present when I spoke to WO Clime, and he could see how upset the Colonel was. At that the CO turned and left to his quarters and was not seen until the evening briefing. (The date was June 19, 1969 when the six men died and the four aircraft men were all members of Company C, 229th Aviation).

The rest of our stay at Camp Gorvad was uneventful. From here we were flown to an LZ whose name I have forgotten but not the wet and miserable time we had there. At this forgotten LZ it rained every day we were there and we would walk from hooch to hooch in the mud. It was not unusual to fall several times in the mud as we maneuvered within the LZ. When we picked up our plate of chow it was full of water by the time we arrived at where we would eat it.

Then we went to build another LZ which would be named O'Keefe in honor of our S-3 that had been killed in the Huey incident. O'keefe was out side a Vietnamese village and on a hillside, not a hilltop as was normal. It was surrounded by thick jungle vegetation but with the aid of the heavy machinery from the Sea Bees we cleared the area. Outside of LZ O'keefe one of our companies (D Company) had contact with a big NVA unit and lost four men Larry Garner, Richard Lee Hardesty, Leonard Louis Alvarado and John Morrison Mahoney. Sp4 Alvarado was an M-60 gunner who had killed many enemy soldiers before they overran his machine gun position. The next LZ would be named after him.

So we got word to move from LZ O'Keefe to LZ Alvarado which was inside a small village and there we were to be augmented by South Vietnamese Army soldiers. The fun came when we tried to move to Alvarado. I ordered all the Chinooks to move the men and supplies and even some Cranes to move the petroleum containers to Alvarado. The S-3 Huey which I rode in went to drop of some soldiers that were helping me with the evacuation. When the last crane came in I had to hook up the rubber container underneath the big crane. As I did this the overcast sky began to close in and as I picked up my radio I heard my Huey say he was turning back because of bad weather.

Holy smoke! I was all alone on an empty LZ with only my radio, my Car-15, and my pistol and grenades. I did not have food or water but most of all no friendly soldiers and I was in enemy territory. I knew I had to act fast so I started to look for any food, water or extra ammo that might have been left behind by our men. I was able to locate six grenades so I gathered my personnel belongings and looked for a good bunker covering the direction from which I felt the enemy might come.

All of a sudden I saw movement in the jungle in front of me. I spread out my grenades and magazines and even pull out my pistol. I darted another look toward the movement and now there was a lot of movement. Certainly they had seen me but why was no one firing in my direction. This was like the scene in Bataan (the movie) in which Robert Taylor was surrounded by *Japs*. I was going to live my own Bataan even if it was for a short time. Another look toward the wood line an now I could see hundreds of soldiers coming at me.

I braced my self for the worst. I picked up my rifle and switched it on fully auto and looked for a command group. Might as well kill the command element since in the reloading phase I felt sure they would take me out. The soldiers continued advancing toward me and I could see a mob of battalion size in the open and coming closer. Now they were less than one hundred meters away and very much in range of my Car-15. I felt somewhat disappointed but glad that these enemy soldiers could not see me and were not shooting.

All of a sudden out of nowhere I heard in perfect English "Don't shoot we are Americans". The only thing American was the voice for I could see the soldiers' faces and they were *Gooks*. "Don't shoot were Americans" came the voice again, and now they were about thirty meters away. At that time the soldiers sat down and three men were left standing and they proceeded toward me. "Where did you come from", one of the men asked. "Did your unit leave you behind", he continued.

"Stop! Don't move or I will shoot", I shouted. "Are you going to shoot three American Army Advisors when you are surrounded by four hundred Cambodian Mercenaries who have been watching you for several hours from the tree line"? At that time all three men broke out in laughter. They were all American advisors and they had three companies of Cambodian Mercenaries under their control. With one hand movement the Cambodians surrounded the area I was in and settled down. They quickly built a fire and started preparations to cook a wild pig they were towing with them.

All night long I talked to these men who were eager to know what was going on and why I had been left behind by my unit. They seemed to enjoy my company and I knew I was not going to sleep at all that

175

night. In the morning the Huey came and took me to LZ Alvarado and I said good by to my new friends. As the Huey lifted I could see the Advisors scrambling the mercenaries to head back to the jungle. I knew my new friends had a story to tell and I certainly had one.

I spent about one more week at LZ Alvarado and then I received a letter from the Army that I had been accepted at Laredo Junior College for the Fall 69 Semester and would be awarded an early out to be home for the semester. One day LTC Boone had a hasty awards presentation and presented me with a Silver Star, a couple of Bronze Stars, a couple of Air Medals, a Purple Heart, an Army Commendation Medal, a Combat Infantry Badge and all the other campaign and service medals that went with the tour of duty in Viet-Nam.

I left the field at LZ Alvarado and went to Quan Loi to clear my unit. I went to the mess hall for lunch and I was so excited about going home that a piece of roast beef got trapped in my throat as I was talking non-stop. I could feel getting short of breath and about to pass out when one of the soldiers on my table gave me a whack on my neck and it dislodged the piece of beef. I almost chocked on a piece of meat after going through all the adventures in the field.

I went to Ben Hoa and processed out of the 1st Cav and it was very smooth as the clerk (Spec 4 Linda) had been my soldier in Basic Training at Fort Bliss. I was driven to Long Binh and there I boarded a Tiger Airlines jet to fly to Oakland, California. When we arrived at the terminal at Oakland we were greeted by the famous hecklers with their insults and other nonsense, but we quickly learned to ignore them. What a great feeling it was to be home after that tour of duty. It was great to be back in the United States of America. Those people shouting insults to us should go try for themselves being outside the U.S. and in a hostile environment and see how they would feel The great feeling came from just ignoring them.

In Oakland we were processed out as I had no desire to remain in the service. I figured one tour of duty was enough for everyone. One tour of duty with the 1st Cavalry Division was enough for a lifetime, and when I had left for Viet-Nam I was twenty-one years old but now at twenty-two I felt as if I was forty.

I'm very proud to have served in the United States Army and elated to have gone to war with the 1st Air Cavalry.

CHAPTER 32

Back in the USA

In Oakland I quickly called my sister Ofelia who was living in Hayward, California a few miles away. Carlos, her husband was working at the Hunts Cannery there in Hayward, so she and her girls Nora and Nelda came to pick me up. After a few meals with them I headed for Ft. Sam Houston where my release from the Army would be ready for me but when I arrived they told me it would be another ten days before it was ready. I had some leave time so I took it and left for Laredo via bus line. I was asked to reconsider staying in since I was due for a promotion to Captain in a few days. I asked if I could return to Ft. Bliss but was told that there was a slot for me at Ft. Jackson, so I quickly said no and asked to be released.

I arrived in Laredo and Linda and her mother were at the bus station waiting for me. Her father was at home preparing a small reception for me. When we got to her home besides her Dad and little sister Elsa there were a few other people there. Those at the reception were Jose Rodriguez and his wife Judy, Derly Ramirez and his wife Lupita, Ramiro Nix and his wife Beatriz. Others there were Jesus Garcia and his wife Blanca, and Oscar Lopez and his wife Jeanie. All made me feel good to be home.

The next morning I jump started my 1964 Pontiac Lemans and headed for Sabinas to see my parents and other family. My brothers Gregorio and Roberto were in Ft. Wayne working for the year and I would not see them until the winter. Dad took me immediately to the ranch as he was anxious to show me what had happened while I was gone. The horse that had thrown me was dead from the aftermath of a hurricane and that was good news. He had some watermelons hidden in some weeds that he had being saving for me at the ranch. They were heavy black diamonds and by the time I got them from the field to the pick up I had lost my appetite for watermelons. He took me to the mountains to look for honey, and after a dozen or so bites from the bees, I also was in no mood to eat some.

I returned to Laredo and enrolled at Laredo Junior college and started my college career. After being out of school for three years it was hard for me to get used to going to class and doing homework and research at night. Linda had I decided to get married and we set a date for December 20, 1969. Linda had recently graduated from Beauty School and had a small shop behind her parents home.

I was receiving Veterans Benefits to attend school but I soon found out it would not be enough to carry the household finances. I rented a backyard garage apartment from Mrs. Perez Garcia a very nice teacher with three kids whose husband was a businessman. One day her son Luis was playing with firecrackers and made me dive under the bed thinking it was incoming.

About this time Ramiro Nix who had been the Commander of the 850th Collection and Classification Company of the Army Reserve in Laredo paid me a visit and asked me to join the Company. By the time I said yes he had been replaced by Capt Royle Wright a local insurance and real estate man.

Soon our wedding day arrived and Linda and I were married at Holy Redeemer Church. We had a morning reception at the Elks Lodge and then everyone headed for Sabinas for an evening reception and dance. SGT John Perkins came down from Liberty, Texas and was my best man. After a short honeymoon to New Orleans, La. and a visit to John Perkins and his parents in Liberty we returned to Laredo. I got a job selling light fixtures for American Standard Light Company, and attended Laredo Junior College.

Selling is tough but selling lights and light fixtures was even tougher. My boss was a kind elderly man named Dewey Coats from San Antonio and he never gave up on me trying his best to teach me a ruff business.

Eventually I moved on to sell world Book Encyclopedia and that proved to be harder than the light fixtures. Finally, I landed a job with Dial Financial Corporation. The job consisted of collecting on old debts and screening customers wishing new loans.

This job proved to be O.K. and the office was managed by a man named Moises Terrazas but it was the Assistant Manager Juan Castillo that I struck a relationship with. Juan and I had some things in common like we were both Viet-Nam Veterans and belonged to the same Army Reserve Unit and suffered the same aches and pains from the war. Soon he and his wife Juanita had a baby girl and Linda and I baptized her and therefore became her god-parents.

I managed to stay with Dial for eighteen months and got along well with their regional supervisor, Billy Shelton, even though he was a pressure cooker when it came to the financial business. Meanwhile Juan and I would find some fun out of a hard line of work. It was inconceivable what people did to get out of paying their monthly account.

On several occasions we had to reposes their personal property to get them to pay their bills. There were many times that people would not open their doors even thought we knew they were there, much like when the Jehovah Witnesses or Mormons come calling. Many people pretended not to know you when they met us in the streets, so when they came to the office and we knew they needed more money we pretended not to see them waiting.

Meanwhile, Capt Wright had accepted a position in Houston and Lt. Boone Lagrange had decided to continue his life as a farmer in the Rio Grande Area so I assumed command of the unit. I was accompanied by Lt. Pete Lara and Lt. Baldomero Puig in the reserve company. I had other officers such as W.O. Manuel Elizondo, W.O. Orlando Reyes and W.O.Emilio Aldape. I later picked up Lt. Jose F. Rodriguez a Viet-Nam Veteran and Lt. Javier Montemayor, a returnee from Germany. A funnier man than Montemayor I could not have found, and he also played the guitar and sang, which came in handy during the long summer camps especially at Ft. Hood.

After eighteen months with Dial I left to accept a job as manager of a social agency named Manpower, Education, and Training. I was highly recommended by a man who had been in charge of the Texas Employment Commission, Ralph Garcia Sr. Ralph was a highly respected man in the Labor field and somehow had taken me under his wings. This program was sponsored by Department of Labor and was designed in getting farm labor migrants out of the migrant stream and into more steady employment in the industry especially in East Texas. In Louisiana the program targeted poor unemployable blacks and placed them in more productive obs.

Although we had three board members that lived in our area my program supervisors were two men, one was Ventura Rios and the other was a man named Acosta. My board members were Mr. Jose Quintanilla, Mr. Garcia, and Mr. Roland Nunez and they represented our interests on the board. The organization was called MET for short was housed at 201 Market Street in Laredo and there the offices and classrooms were located. The local office consisted of a secretary who was Diana Butterfield later replaced by Maria Hernandez. We had a local recruiter (Fidel Garza) who went around the city looking for new participants for the program. We had a counselor (Arturo Villarreal) who made sure the families qualified for the program under Dept of labor guidelines. There were two instructors who each had their classroom. One was Jose F. Rodriguez (Also in the Army Reserve with me) another Viet-Nam Vet who was the vocational instructor. The other instructor was Lauro Garcia who was the academic instructor. I was the Director of the Program at the Laredo Office and with the staff we numbered six in all.

To qualify for the program and receive the training they had to have been agricultural farm migrants and had participated in actual farm laborer in the past recent months. They must have been willing to leave the migrant stream and accept steady jobs. After, eight weeks of training in Laredo they were transferred to a training site in Goodrich, Texas to finish their training before been placed in steady jobs. While in Goodrich they not only received the monetary stipend, they were also given a place to live.

I worked at this agency for three years until I could not stand working for Rios and Acosta and I resigned. I was replaced by Lauro Garcia the academic instructor. I went on to work for Whittleseys Fine Meats out of Mission Texas but with the Laredo area as my territory. At the same time I started to work for Whittleseys I decided to apply for employment with U.S. Customs because they were federal government but I did not have to carry a weapon at the work site.

In the reserves I was doing well and had been promoted to Captain. My unit had been chosen to train in Germany for sixteen days and it was a good treat for all of us. It was this time that a second baby appeared on the scene as Victor Jr. was born just as we departed to go to Germany. Edmundo Martinez one of my enlisted men in the unit offered to have his wife stay with Linda in those difficult times. They were from Zapata and she was attending Laredo State University and it would work out well for both. They later baptized Victor Jr. for us.

Upon my return from Germany I went to Customs and interviewed with the director Mr. Sewall and after going over my application he offered me a job at Rio Grande, Texas, but first I had to take the entrance exam. I took the exam and went back to Mr. Sewall with my results. Mrs. Sylvia Salinas took me to see the director and what a surprise. He said he was sorry but he could not hire me because I had not passed the test as I had gotten a 69 on it. I had read the exam and to me the score read 79% but that included the 10 points for Veterans Preference and the Purple Heart. Oh, how embarrassing. He advised me to take it over, and I did, but this time I received a 35%. Goodbye U.S. Customs.

One day while I was still selling institutional foods and fine meats for Whittleseys I was told the Border Patrol Test was coming up and if I wanted to take it and I said—NO! I did not want to carry a gun for any one again. That night Linda and I were going to dinner and talk about it when outside her parents home there was a confrontation between a drunk and a policeman. With both of us in the background of the bad guy they stood there and emptied their handguns at each other.

After making sure that Linda was not hit, I went to the aid of the policeman. Both the officer and the drunk were there reloading to start shooting again when I walked up to the drunk pushed him over and took the gun away from him. The drunk had been hit by Officer's Flores (El Talache) bullets so he fell down when I pushed him and never got up. I helped the Officer until help arrived and Linda and I went to have supper.

One day Linda's grand father Tomas Garcia who had retired from a career with the U.S. Border Patrol and the Immigration Service was sitting on a bench outside Linda's parents small drive in store and gave me some free advice. In his usual way of talking, he said to me, "Quit wasting time and join the Border Patrol, you are going to regret it later". Mr. Garcia had been a legendary agent from the first class of Border Patrol Agents in 1925. He was used to people doing what he said and to not do it would bring the Irish temper out in him. There was no need to wake up the percentage of Irish blood the man was carrying.

Picture of Don Tomas Garcia in his INS uniform
when he was OIC at the Port of Roma.

The next day I went to the Border Patrol Office and applied to take the test. The day came soon enough and the day before the test I was changing my mind about the Border Patrol so I went to a family outing and had a few beers. The next day was a Saturday and the test was at the main Post Office. Well, I overslept that day and decided to go tell them I was not going to take the test.

When I arrived there I was greeted by Mrs. Castro the tester and I told her I was not going to test because I did not feel good. She looked at me and said "Go get some coffee, the tests did not arrive yesterday and we are waiting for Mr. Palacios the Postmaster to come and open the special mail and see if the tests are there". The tests were in and I sat down to take the test and make the best out of a bad situation.

I quickly received my score and I had scored a 99% plus I still had my ten extra points for the Veterans Preference and Purple Heart Medal. Now the background checks and medical exams were next followed by an interview and then just wait for a hiring date. I still was not sure about the Border Patrol and carrying a gun again. Well, I guess we will cross that river later. Soon I received a letter to report to Laredo Sector on November 15, 1975. Wow! Six years had passed since returning from Viet-Nam.

When I received my scores I went outside our house and there was a Border Patrol Agent fixing an old Chevy truck. He was always there when he was not working. It was Gerald Tisdale and a very nice Agent that did not have his family here yet and spent most of his time working on the truck. He advised me to go to the Academy but that the less they knew about my military the better. Soon Brenda and their two kids showed up and they moved to a bigger house. Gerry had been a prior service Agent and was one of the better marksman I would meet in the Border Patrol.

I NO HERO Part 11

My Border Patrol Career

CHAPTER 33

The Border Patrol in Laredo, Texas

Well, here I was back home in Laredo in our own home at 2015 Chihuahua, an older home I had purchased and it was very comfortable. Linda had a beauty shop in the back where an old garage had been. It had a large yard and the two kiddos would run around most of the day as Linda did her beauty work.

I reported to Laredo Border Patrol Station which at that time was the only Border Patrol Station (LRN) and of course there was the Laredo Sector HQ (LRT) offices there also at 201 Del Mar Boulevard. My first assignment was on the evening shift (4PM to 12PM) under a supervisor named Gordon Aker.

Gordon Aker was a very nice older man who had acquired the nickname of "Pappy" and he was well liked by everyone in the rank and file. He also had the grandpa look with little or no hair on his head. All in all he was a good man and a good supervisor. He quickly assigned to a journeyman named Jimmy McNair. McNair was a petite cowboy type, and very nice fellow. What Jimmy lacked in size he made up with a go getter attitude.

The first night things were pretty slow until Pappy Acker called us and said there was a trail on the sensor board on the east highline near H-359. The sensors indicated that three aliens were moving along the highline and headed east toward Lake Casa Blanca. As we traveled Jimmy told me to make the challenge to the aliens and he would get behind them in case they ran. He did not tell me what the challenge was so I made one up. Soon, we could hear the aliens talking as they came down the highline. When they were about ten feet away I stepped out from behind the bushes and said " Buenas Noches Senores" as I fired three rounds from my Colt Trooper into the night air. The aliens jumped out of their *"Guaraches"* very much as the Viet-Nameese had humped out of the Ho Chi Ming Slicks back in Nam. In seconds they were gone running back toward Mexico without their footwear. We had apprehended three sets of *"guaraches"* and that was all. A very embarrassed Jimmy McNair stepped out of the shadows and said "What did you do that for"?

We reported back to Sector and Pappy quickly asked "Did you guys already processed the aliens and Volunteer Returned them back to Mexico". Jimmy found his voice and told him what had happened. Pappy took a look at me and I new I was fired on my first day, instead he went to his thermo jug filled up a small cup of what ever he had in the jug, drank it nonstop and said "You are going to be a handful".

Soon I started to work with other journeymen some more colorful that others. There was an Anglo agent by the name of Jay Calk that acted like he was always mad, but he wasn't. Once you got him talking and laughing, he was a great guy. There was a plumb looking agent named Robert Randle who walked so slow everyone called him "Bullet Bob" but he was super nice. There was a giant of a man named Clifford Green who was a pilot and how he managed to get into those small planes was a wonder. This man was a good six foot four inches and a had big broad shoulders. Then there was Dennis Cogburn who was always gripping and fretting about something or other. When the chips were down Dennis had a way of coming through as he had been in several shootouts with bad guys and had always come out the winner.

Then there was our post academy trainer J.W. Clifford who would instruct us one day a week and you could always tell when he was mad because he was bald and his head would turn red, like a light bulb, a big one. When Clifford was mad at us (trainees) he would put us in a van and then go show us the territory, on the bumpiest roads until someone would—vomit.

One day as we worked the Galvan Fence looking for brush walkers we got into a argument that he got so upset that instead of spitting into his spittoon he drank from it causing all kinds of heybuck with his intestines—he off course blamed me for his troubles. In the patrol the new guy always got blamed for whatever goes wrong and you learn to live with it. Should I say more? There was Ken Sanderfer who could have played Jeremiah Johnson in the movie as he looked like Robert Redford on most days.

There were other colorful individuals, two of these were Jesse Martinez and Cecilio Ruiz. These two guys had joined the Border Patrol early and were sort of seniors among the rest of us. They were both good workers although Jesse was sort of calm compared to Cecilio. Cecilio was a big bruiser looking guy who could have been a bouncer at any club. Cecilio transferred to Kingsville and later was shot in the buttocks by a drug smuggler dressed as a priest. There was another old timer named Joe Galvan, but he kept to himself most of the time.

Perhaps the most colorful of the journeymen or old timers was a man named Dale Squint. This agent loved to work the river and was always uncovering some activity on the river banks. When I reported in to Laredo and had to be licensed in a government vehicle he took me for a test drive or spin. When I got into the vehicle I quickly noticed that this was indeed the same man that had made the accident report on the bus rollover near Sierra Blanca when I was in the Army and the soldiers had been killed. At that time he was with the Texas Department of Public Safety as a Trooper---small world indeed.

The supervisors at Laredo Station (now Laredo North) besides Pappy were also pretty colorful. There was H. Pool whom I worked for and know personally for over thirty years and I still don't know what the H. stands for in his name. Pool was one of those supervisors that stood by their agents and as long as you carried your own weight he was supportive of you. There was an older man named Bill Randolph who looked like a college professor misplaced. He was good to work for but would argue in a short notice.

A colorful supervisor in his own right was Cy Reynolds. This man you could write a book on. One evening the lookout came over the radio that an Army General in San Antonio was found hung at an armory. It was suspected that terrorists had done the awful deed and might be trying to escape into Mexico. We set up roadblocks on highways leading to Mexico and started the searched for the terrorists. We were lacking supervision so we looked for our supervisor who was nowhere to be found.

A search started for our own man which went on till morning when someone heard a radio transmission coming from the back of an old Chevrolet truck with a camper parked outside the station. A search of the camper produced not only the radio but our supervisor also, fast asleep. So mush for our terrorist search, but at least we found our supervisor.

CHAPTER 34

Agent duties at Laredo

Work at Laredo Station for the forty or so agents that we numbered at that time consisted mostly of Traffic Check and Line Watch Operations with some others areas also covered. The Traffic Check which consisted of two to three but mostly two Agents dressed in dress uniform inspecting traffic on the highways leading from Laredo. This was done from a commercial van which was stationed on the side of the highway and the traffic was directed to it by traffic type cones. The major highway was IH-35 and that inspection was held almost always with the exception of bad weather.

Two other highways lead away from Laredo those being H-59 toward Freer and H-359 toward Hebbronville. These inspections points were also held personnel permitting. If there was not enough personnel then there was a "roving patrol" assigned to observed traffic on these highways and inspected any vehicle that aroused suspicion being very careful not to single people out and definitely not violated their rights.

Also if personnel permitted there would be a "back-up' unit of one or two agents assigned to support the checkpoints and work the dirt roads where the checkpoints could be circumvented. These agents would also help out in case the checkpoints got overloaded with arrests especially during holidays. They would also handle transportation of the aliens detained or arrested back to Laredo if there were no detention units available. There was also bus check and train checks that were made under the transportation checks as were the few airlines that departed from Laredo in those days.

Under Line Watch Operations, agents were responsible for the river crossings which ranged from the Zapata County Line to Laredo and then west to the Briscoe Ranch area. This meant the Agents would watch the numerous river crossings for aliens and contraband mainly drugs coming into the country. There was usually a lot of action around the Ports of Entry as most aliens denied to enter the United States would return to Mexico and try to entry surreptitiously.

There were also the many sensor trails to be worked as those aliens that were not arrested at the water's edge made their way north on the many dirt roads and primitive trails, along the electrical high lines and ranch fences. Many of these had been electronically bugged with surplus sensors donated by the military. Much of the ranch land around Laredo is made up of large ranches that came from old Spanish Grants and their fence lines stretch northward from the river since everyone was granted some water rights of the mighty Rio Grande.

The ranchland around Laredo is mostly of low and medium height brush with some areas covered with mesquite. Some of the mesquites do grow to twenty or thirty feet but for the most part they are around ten feet in height. Sometimes in the long summers a good shade is hard to find and causes some serious problems to the aliens trying to get out of the scorching sun. Many perish every year due to the hot sun and lack of good water.

There were other duties for the agents when there were enough of us to go around like Sensor Board Watch which was to monitor the sensors as they lit up when the aliens were moving on a trail that was bugged. Later on details to Prosecutions and Vehicle Seizures were started as the momentum of court cases and seizures started to build up as more agents came into the sector and there fore more production in the number of cases. Occasionally there were details out of our areas to roundup aliens at the large work sites. All in all there was enough work diversity to keep the average agent interested in his new job.

CHAPTER 35

My new career in the U.S. Border Patrol

I did not know it then but I was joining one of the best federal law enforcement agencies that are available in the U.S. Here I would meet some of the best young men in the agency, some as good as the ones I had served with in Viet-Nam, unfortunately I would also meet some of the worst. Some that not only did they not fit in the picture of law enforcement at all, but somehow got into the agency to better their egos and their pockets. It is these persons that have brought the agency down instead of keeping it where it should be.

On November 15, 1975, I reported to Laredo Sector of the U.S. Border Patrol. I was one of two agents to be assigned at their home site. The other was Border Patrol Agent Horacio Vela, who was 21 while I was 28 years of age. There were several other agents assigned at the same time at Laredo. They were Jud Spring, Oscar Barrientes, Juan Soto, Billy Pierce, Larry Boetel, and Ricky Rodriguez. We were hired at the grade of GS-7 and would be attending the Border Patrol Academy and be considered a trainee for one year probationary period. Even after returning from the Academy in Los Fresnos, Texas we would continue to train one day out of the week and have a progress test after 5 1/2 months and then again at ten months. After passing all the requirements we would be Journeymen Border Patrol Agents and be promoted to GS-8.

Training at Los Fresnos was hectic but not impossible. It consisted of an Academic schedule of Spanish, Immigration and Nationality Laws, Criminal Law and Statutory Law and of course physical training and firearms. We lived in some military type dorms with two agents per room. The training site had a nice cafeteria and a small bar-type club. The cafeteria served fairly good meals and the club I had no use for since I was overweight and needed to lose some pounds. I reported in at 245 lbs, and graduated at 190 lbs.

The training was somewhat like the military but in a way it was easier than the military. It consisted of getting up early and doing physical training and then cleaning up for breakfast before going to class. The morning consisted of the routine law classes and then lunch. In the afternoon we usually had Spanish classes and then the running part of the physical training. In the afternoon we usually worked on the famous obstacle course or ran or a combination of both. The running was usually sprints, laps or the 5 mile run to see the Wizard.

The run to see the Wizard was usually the most physical of all since it consisted of running 2.5 miles on an abandoned runway to an abandoned bunker where some funny guy had drawn a wizard on the metal door. Like fools we had to yell out to the wizard to please come out and if he did we could walk the distance back to the dorms. I guess I don't have to tell you the critter never came out and we had to run back to the dorms every time. Then there was the feeling of being a fool for going up to the drawing of the Wizard and begging him to come out. For graduating purposes we only had to run two miles and not the Wizard Run.

The final and most fun of the training was the firearms training. We had to qualify with our sidearm which was a Colt Trooper in 357 Caliber. We had to get familiar with the 870 Shotgun in buckshot and slugs. Some of us also shot with the M-16 which I was very familiar with by now. The obstacle course was a different thing since we had to scale up a rope and go across the monkey bar latter. There was the inclined wall we had to maneuver over and the rope that we had to go across. All in all it was challenging, but it got easier with practice and as my weight got under control.

And so the months went by from November to February. Sometime in January we were taken to practice our new gained knowledge of

Immigration Laws in the fields surrounding Los Fresnos. I was assigned to work in Brownsville on the river banks and near McAllen in the orange groves. One night I reported to Brownsville Border Patrol Station for the evening shift and my assigned journeyman was preparing me for the shift, when a tall blond agent was standing next to me. Jerry Spruiell, a classmate of mine from Martin and a former basketball player was the agent. After the quick hellos we left to go work the Brownsville Bridge that crossed to Matamoros on the Mexican side.

My partner was happy that I had run into Jerry and mentioned to me how Jerry had been an All-State basketball player at Martin. When I did not agree or disagree, he stopped and said "I thought so, he was not, right Vic". I did not answer as I did not now how many feathers Jerry had put on his own hat. Unintentionally, I had unmasked Jerry's claim to fame.

Well, my journeyman stopped by the international bridge and sent me to work underneath the bridge while he went to the coffee shop to tell the others about Jerry not being an All-Stator. Well I went into the darkness under the bridge to arrest aliens. Soon after I heard some scuffling and grunting and realized that aliens were crawling underneath the bridge on a pipe that came all the way across from the Mexican side. The aliens, who some were drunk and some were not were having their problems as the pipe was very cold. Soon they started falling off the pipe but they were already on U.S. soil so I arrested them and placed them behind a dirt pile. Many fell asleep quickly which was good since I only had two pairs of handcuffs. I started to call my partner but he was too busy rubbing Jerry's story at the nearby restaurant to pay attention to me.

Finally, he came to help me and I sent the aliens up the embankment to him. At last I came up and he was surprised. "Where did you get all these aliens", he yelled. "I arrested them coming over on the pipe". "But you arrested twenty-eight aliens down there, that is almost unheard off", he continued. Well the joke was on him because while he was in the coffee shop harassing Jerry, I had arrested the aliens.

The next day the Asst. Patrol Agent in Charge of the Academy called me in since he had heard of my alien arrests. He said he was proud of me and especially because my grandfather was the legendary Tomas Garcia, who had been his supervisor in earlier years. I tried to explain to him that he was my wife's grandfather but I was not very successful. Soon it was all over that the grandson of Tomas Garcia had arrested a large group of aliens single handedly and as a trainee on my first day in the field.

Not all the days at the Academy were cheerful, there were the days we had to run and the costal wind was so strong it seemed to bend our bodies when we ran against it, but when we ran with it on our back we sure ran fast. There were some instructors that were pretty neat others would get lost if it wasn't for their lesson plan. They made the time pass on rapidly.

One day we had an instructor named J.J. Fulghiam and he was a character with a cowboy drawl, it seemed to me he had just stepped out of a Zane Grey Novel. He had been stationed at Eagle Pass Texas and was now a supervisor on his way to Laredo, Texas, after his tour as an instructor. He was teaching us Spanish and he realized that all the class was made up on Spanish speakers so there was little he could teach us. He pulled out some slides and started to show them to us about his exploits in Eagle Pass Station. He got to a picture of a lady standing holding two monstrous dogs on the leach.

The dogs were sitting on their heels while the lady was standing. In the deepest cowboy drawl he said "Fellers, that's my wife----the one that's standing." Since the dogs were sitting and she was the only human in the picture it was taken for granted that the lady was his wife. One trainee laughed and we all joined him, much to the distaste of our instructor. By the time we finished laughing, he had put up the projector and slides. "What you fellers need is to learn to run," and he was a little mad. That afternoon we Ran, Ran, Ran, until it was not funny anymore. From then on no one laughed in his Spanish class. And when I reported to Laredo he was there and for a long time I did not laugh.

At times life was hectic at the Border Patrol Academy studying for the Exams and working on the Physical Training and then there was my family in Laredo and the Army Reserve in San Antonio. Ever thing had to fall in place. Every week end Horacio and I would travel to see our families in my little Toyota station wagon. We would split the four dollars of gas the little s/w would use between Laredo and Los Fresnos.

One day Linda miss carried our third child and I was sent home. The stress levels were too high on her carrying the household by herself. After a few days she felt better and asked me to return to the Academy. She knew that I was trying to qualify for a better job and a better future for the entire family. In February of 1976 we finally graduated from the U.S. Border Patrol Academy. I had done well losing over fifty pounds of weight and looking and feeling much better. Now I had to go through the post academy training and wait out my probation period.

Chapter 36

Jim Turner and the alien baby

The work at Laredo Station was usually varied and an agent like myself usually worked with a senior man even if senior by only a year or so. I was lucky to work with some journeymen that went out and taught me things that I needed to know in this federal law enforcement business. I knew how to shoot and defend myself as the Army had trained me well, but this was different since I just could not shoot everybody. I had to be careful and use common sense etc.

One of the journeyman that I was lucky to work with was a young man I nicknamed Mr. Handsome because of his looks, his name was Loren Wilkins. He had joined the Border Patrol after a short stint with the Texas Highway Patrol. One evening he was having me stop vehicles on IH-35 when he directed me to stop a car going in the opposite direction. Being new at the business I made a quick turn around going over the cement median and flicked the overhead lights on the car.

The Agent observed as I got out of the patrol cruiser approached the car and carefully inspected the passengers. When I returned he had a smile and said that was well done except " you went over the median without regard for the cruiser and you almost high centered the car" and he went on and on. He said that as I turned even sparks were flying from the car coming in contact with the cement median. "That was the roughest turned around I have ever witnessed", he went on. From that day on I was very careful on my turnarounds no matter who was with me. He said "You have to glide thru your turns and make it very smooth and professional", he had said enough.

Another evening I was assigned to my old friend Dale Squint and we observing traffic on IH-35 since it was drizzling and the Check-Point was not operational. A pick-up passed our location and Squint quickly became energized and said "Stop that Truck". But I could not see any probable cause to stop it, since there was only one occupant in the truck and it did not appear to be heavily loaded.

When the truck stopped he said to place the driver under arrest and I became more curios what was going on. I asked "Why" and he answered because the truck was stolen. I became more curios since I had not even called in the plates to our radio room. Well, I did and the license plates showed the truck was stolen. I was possessed to find out how he knew the truck was stolen so I pressed for an answer. He said "Look at the back license plate how it is full of bugs, well that plate must have been on the front of another vehicle since bugs don't hit the back license plates",---close this case on experience lots of experience!

There were other interesting officers on the highways besides the Border Patrol Agents. One evening while working the traffic check point on IH-35 a very drunk driver approached the inspection station. He was an Anglo man who worked at a tractor test site down the road. I could tell he was very drunk and a danger to anyone on the highway. I asked him to park his car on the side of the highway and wait for my instructions. I called for a Texas Highway Patrol Unit to check him out.

A highway patrol unit arrived within minutes and a six foot four officer stepped out of the cruiser. It was Raymond Earl Garner the tallest officer in the Laredo Highway Patrol Office. I accompanied him to the car with the drunk driver. When Garner tapped on the window with his metallic flashlight the drunk woke up but upon seeing the uniformed highway patrol officer he pretended to go back to sleep. This cat and mouse went on several times until Garner smashed the window with his flashlight and pulled the driver out thru the window. The drunk was now fully awake and kept yelling " I was playing with you officer". Patrolman Garner calmly answered " I was not".

One early morning I was working with a Journeymen named Jim Turner. We were working the ranches near Encinal this one being the

Vidales Ranch which sits off IH-35 and the aliens use it to parallel the main highway and continue their trek North. It was a nice spring morning but we knew it would be hot soon. We uncovered a small group of tracks headed toward Encinal of two adults and a child by the size of the tracks on the morning moist soil.

We followed them for several miles and we took turns moving the Ram Charger forward as not to get caught too far from it when it got hotter. It was my turn to move the utility vehicle as Jim entered an arroyo that was covered with vegetation and trees. He was in there for a few minutes and I could hear him talking so I parked the vehicle and walked over to the arroyo. Jim came out with a small family consisting of a man and a woman and a small girl. But the most amusing thing was that Turner who was usually a serious person came out with a naked little Mexican baby mounted on his shoulders. He looked at me and said "Vic, one of my kids recently married and do you think I'm going to look good as a grandpa".

I started to laugh and said "Yes, Jim your going to look pretty good, but that kid has the runs and he just did all over your shirt and badge"!

Border Patrol Agent Victor M. Villarreal with nine illegal aliens shortly after entering the U.S. near the water plant at Laredo.

CHAPTER 37

The Old Smuggler and I

One evening I was working sensors with a young agent named Bill Mitchell who since then has moved on to the IRS agency. We were working alien trails headed north from Laredo toward Encinal, Texas at night. There had been a lot of traffic near Encinal and it was suspected that an alien smuggler from Colombia, Nuevo Leon, Mexico was doing most of the smuggling since he apparently knew the area very well and could travel it any time of day or night. This smuggler was known for his huge tennis shoe prints in the soft soil and had acquired the nickname of "Big Foot".

I was given the assignment by Supervisor Gordon Acker "Pappy" to track this smuggler down until he was arrested and to set the man up for prosecutions. Bill and I made our cuts (search for tracks) in certain areas where this smuggler had frequented and had worked his way up around the IH-35 Checkpoint area. No one knew what the man or woman looked like but we had a good idea of what shoes he wore by the pattern his tennis were leaving on the trials.

BPA Villarreal at a dugout made by the aliens to avoid
detection near the Check Point on IH-35.

It was almost midnight and toward the end of our normal evening
shift when Gordon Acker advised us that there was some activity on
the electrical high line headed for Encinal. Whether this was our target
or not we decided to give it a shot at capturing the aliens. We hopped
onto an old van I was driving and headed toward Encinal in hopes of
getting in front of the aliens.

According (because of the activity on the sensor board) to the
supervisor they were still moving and they were staying under the
electrical line. Bill and I were able to get ahead of the group according
to the time element the sensors were denoting on the sensor board back
at the office. I advised Bill to get into position behind the group and I
would make the challenge. As the group got close and we could hear
them talking we turned off our walkie-talkies as sound travels a long
way at night.

As the group got closer I could hear the voices distinctly and under
stand every word they said. I could hear an alien ask another how long
he had been doing this and the other replied for about thirty years.

OH! This was the voice of the smuggler. He went on to say that Border Patrolmen were so stupid they had never been able to catch him because he was slick and knew the area better than the agents.

The smuggler went on and on insulting the agents and the U.S. Government for not been able to apprehend him. Meanwhile I was getting enraged by this man's insults although not directed at me in particular. I sneaked behind a telephone pole which at that time hid most of my body and waited. As the boisterous individual came abreast with the pole that I was hiding behind, I threw a punch with my right fist and knocked him down as Bill stepped up and captured the group. The party was not over as the smuggler sprung to his feet and went on the offensive punching and kicking me until after a few minutes I was able to subdue him and handcuff him.

We placed the group in the van and headed for Laredo. I radioed ahead and informed Gordon Acker I had the notorious "Big Foot" in custody. He was elated that we had put the famous smuggler out of business and waited for our arrival sipping on his "Coffee". We arrived in Laredo and Bill unloaded the contents of the van. Acker was curious who the smuggler was but the man that had the handcuffs on and the only one that was handcuffed was an old man about eighty years old and he showed signs of a struggle.

"Get serious Vic, is this the famous Big Foot", he asked? "Yes Pappy, that's him". "Are you going to take that old man tomorrow in front of Marcel Notzon the Federal Magistrate, he's going to laugh you out of the courtroom," he continued? "Get rid of him before he dies in our custody of old age" he continued. The next day I had a bruise on the face where the eighty year old man had punched me during the battle. We never saw his tracks again but I always wondered how old he really was!

Pilot Tom Moss and BPA Glen Simpson with LOH in background.

CHAPTER 38

The Goat Man Incident

One evening I was working line watch with Guadalupe Rodriguez (Wally) and we were assigned the downriver area known as the Richter Farm. The Richter Farm was owned by an Anglo family that lived on the riverbanks of the Rio Grande. For years they had and still do a small farm with irrigational rights from the river. Across from the farm and to the South is a small housing area and several dozen families lived there.

One of the families living there were a woman and man team that owned a small goat herd that they herded on the river edge to graze from the lush vegetation on the river Vega (the Vega is a track of land about fifty feet wide that is considered government land and is available for people to use for fishing, picnicking etc). They had being doing this for several years and I always suspected that they were lookouts for the smugglers notifying them when we were near so they could cease their illegal activities.

The location for these lookouts was excellent since smugglers could load up their cars as a road led all the way to the edge of the river and then they could be back on H-83S within minutes and gone. A person could make a fortune just acting as a lookout for the bad guys. The goats were just a ruse for the couple to be out there and not be so obvious.

That afternoon as Wally and I neared the turnoff off H-83S toward the river we were stopped by a man completely soaked and a small boy also wet. The man identified himself as a Webb County Deputy who was off duty and had been fishing with his son at the river's edge when he was approached by a man herding some goats that asked him to leave the area. The deputy who was not in uniform informed him that he was not going to leave as it was public land and he intended to have a good time with his son.

At that time the Goat man picked up the small boy and threw him into the river. The deputy jumped in to retrieve his son but when he came out of the river the man and the goats were gone. The Deputy advised me that he was going home to drop his boy off and get his gun. I told him to take his boy home and stay there and Wally and I would deal with the Goat man.

I opened the trunk of the cruiser and retrieved my assigned pump shotgun and placed it on my lap as I drove down to where the Goat Man lived. As I drove up to the little house where the man and his wife lived I noticed the goats were already penned up in the corrals next to the house, and this was a good indication that the man was home. I honked the horn of the patrol unit until the man came out of the house.

This man was very crude and had a bad disposition so he came out mad. He took one look at me and started yelling "What the hell do you want Villarreal" he yelled. "I want to talk to you", I responded. I noticed his right hand was behind his body as if he had something, presuming a gun in his hand. "I have nothing to talk to you about, and if you push me, I have a big surprise for you," he continued yelling. I kept my hand on the shot gun which was out of his sight. Out of the corner of my eye I could see Wally moving around as if trying to get out of the car, and he was completely pale.

The Goat Man continued his advance toward me still keeping his right hand out of sight. "You better get out of here and do it fast" he said. At that time I raised the barrel of the shotgun just enough to clear the window and the man saw it. "My God", he yelled, "You are trying to kill me". "OH, please don't shoot, I did not mean to do what I did", he confessed. He quickly pulled out his right hand to show he had nothing there and started to go back into the house. I knew this was the time for me to play Wyatt Earp.

I told the man "This river is not big enough for both of us, and I am not going anywhere so it has to be you, you understand". He nodded his head as he entered the shack. I drove off but noticed my partner was a complete different color. I returned to the office to make my report but Wally was out of the car in a flash. He went straight to Gordon Aker and blurted "Pappy, Victor was almost in a shoot out with the Goat Man, I think Victor wanted to kill the man, I don't want to work with Victor anymore". Pappy Acker did what he always did, he went to pour himself some "Coffee".

The following day I went straight to the Goat Man's house and he and his wife and the goats were gone and were never seen again there. The next week the Goat Man's wife was intercepted at the Port of Entry riding in a taxicab and the Inspectors got suspicious and searched her purse and found a loaded .45 caliber pistol and 77 thousand dollars cash in it. Both the money and the pistol were seized and she disappeared into Mexico.

Sometime later the rumor started that I had killed the Goat Man and eaten his goats.

CHAPTER 39

The Border Patrol without gas

The Border Patrol now enjoys a pretty good budget but it was not always that way. During the Carter Administration years our budget was pretty slim, and one could only wonder if the Border Patrol enforcement had fallen in a bad light. The budget was cut in every one of our departments especially our operating gas fund. Instead of having the normal eight to ten units going out per shift it was usually one van with eight to ten agents in it. The driver of the van would go to one specific location on the river, usually a high point out there and unload the agents. The agents would then patrol on foot along the river in a high visibility mode.

The agents could not really apprehend anyone since removing them was almost impossible. Normally the Agents would walk along the river banks to obviously be seen from the other side and even wave at the aliens who were waiting to cross to the U.S. side. It was almost impossible to do our duties of patrolling the river and therefore safeguarding our country. Sometimes we would build fires on the U.S. side just to show the intruders we were still there. We were fortunate that one of our Agents, Mickey Johnson lived on a rent house on the tallest hill overlooking the Rio Grande and we could park the government van at his house and from there fan out on foot.

It was a hell of a way to run the most powerful government agency on the border—but we lived through it.

CHAPTER 40

The night of the fat bimbos

One evening I was assigned to work back-up to the H-59 checkpoint near Freer, Texas. That afternoon my wife had given me a K-light flashlight for a gift and I was proudly sporting it on my pistol belt. It was a good size flashlight that required four batteries and was a bit longer than most. I did not have a partner so my supervisor and good friend Jim Treviño rode with me. He was concerned about me working alone so far from Laredo and he also wanted to talk to the agents assigned checkpoint duty that evening.

As we neared the checkpoint location on H-59 and FM2050 we noticed a large sedan unloading a group of aliens so that they could walk around the checkpoint. These would normally be picked up on the eastern side of the checkpoint and then be taken east toward Houston, Texas. I drove past the location of the sedan and then turned off my lights and turned the cruiser back west toward Laredo.

Soon we observed the target sedan turn west toward Laredo also. We knew that they had dropped the load for the trek around the Checkpoint and now they would drive west and park until the aliens made it around the Checkpoint. Then they would go east of the Checkpoint and pick the aliens up several hours later.

In order to have a good prosecutable case I decided to stop the car and identify the occupants and Jim agreed. I quickly caught up with the older car and flicked my overhead lights and the car pulled over on the grassy shoulder. As I approached the car I noticed two huge fat men sitting in the front seat. They looked like two big humpy dumpys and must have weighted over four hundred pounds each. Out of the corner of my eye I noticed Jim Treviño approaching the passenger side carefully.

As I was abreast with the driver and asked him for his immigration status, he opened the door and struck me about the knees with the car door. The huge man came out of the car swinging and proceeded to land several punches on me. I grabbed him and down we went rolling in the grass and both punching and kicking as we went. Soon it became evident that my punches were not doing much to subdue "Bluto" and I needed help. Where was my partner and supervisor Jim Treviño.

I finally remember my new metallic flashlight and pulled it out and proceeded to pound the big man's head with it. It took several blows before he eased up on his offensive and I was able to handcuff him in front since there was no way the cuffs were going to fit on his back side. Now, I had this guy under control, but where was my friend Jim Treviño.

I heard some grunting from the passenger side of the car and ran over to find the other fat boy wrestling with Jim on the grass. I ran over to assist Jim as I could see that he had his hands full with bimbo number two. I grabbed my K-light and demolished what was left of it on the man's head and Jim was able to handcuff him. All the time I kept thinking these fat boys were going to kill us, and normally alien smugglers don't go that far to mess with Border Patrol Agents.

I did not know what have driven the fat bimbos to such measures in dealing with us. We booked them for assault of a Federal Officer since we never caught the aliens in the brush. It had been a close call and I wanted to know why. Instead of waiting for my evening shift I went in the next morning and called Federal Probation Supervisor Bobby Adame and told him what had happened. He laughed and said "Vic, both of those "gordos" were on ten years probation and that's why they did not want to get arrested". I told him I would have the paperwork ready in a couple of hours and he said "Don't hurry those guys have violated the conditions of their probation and are not going anywhere for the next ten years."

CHAPTER 41

The night of the fire

One night I was working in the city of Laredo with a quiet agent named Jose Mungia and we were patrolling the area of Laredo known as the Miracle Candle Neighborhood. Joe who normally did not speak unless spoken too was pretty cheerful that evening and we were getting along just fine. All of a sudden I saw smoke coming out of a small house on one of the streets.

I stopped the Border Patrol unit and stepped out the vehicle to get a good look. All of a sudden I heard children crying and I quickly ascertained that they were in the house. I yelled at Mungia to call the Laredo Fire Department as I ran to the door but realized it was locked. I backed up and ran forward putting my right shoulder into the door and it opened wide.

I was received by a cloud of smoke, heat and more children crying. I had to act and act fast as the children in the house did not have long to live in the heat. I wondered where the parents were but I did not have time to look for them. I grabbed the children one at a time and ran outside and handed them to Mungia at the patrol car. At that time Dennis Cogburn showed up as he had heard Mungia's radio transmission and request for help.

When I had the children out of the house now almost completely engulfed in flames and Mungia and Cogburn were trying to comfort them, the Laredo Fire Department arrived and they had brought an

211

ambulance. The children were placed in the ambulance and they took off toward Mercy Hospital. It is a good thing that I decided to follow the ambulance as it broke down a few blocks away and the children were transferred to our patrol unit for the remainder of the trip to the hospital.

I know one of the children died at the hospital because of his burns but the others made it. I realized that the children had been left locked in their house while the parents went somewhere. I guess the parents have to live with their conscious but Mungia, Cogburn and I felt good knowing we had done a good deed. The local TV Station KGNS made a small news show showing us as heros, but we did not feel that way, we were glad to have been there at the right time to help.

CHAPTER 42

Rudy and the Aliens

Checking the freight trains for aliens was never my favorite duty. It involved boarding the trains especially when they were on the move and checking for the aliens. Normally we would start the shift by checking the river crossing and sometimes following the tracks all the way into the hiding places that the aliens used before boarding the train. As departure time got closer the aliens would mass up to rush the train sometimes causing harm to themselves or to the agents who were trying to get them off.

This evening I was assigned a young man who later would work with me on many occasions. His name was Rudy Lopez and all thought he grew up in San Antonio, Texas his Spanish was terrible to say the least, but he was a very pleasant fellow. We were working an area called Jefferson Crossing on the western side of Laredo near the Rio Grande. This area is one of the busiest areas because of the proximity of the freight trains and the abundance of hiding places for the aliens to hide.

Somehow Rudy and I split up looking for fresh sign of aliens as they made their way toward the railroad and the open boxcars. Before I knew it Rudy was completely out of my sight but I did not worry too much as it was still daylight. Rudy's voice come over on the wakie talky and informed me that he had intercepted a group of twelve aliens and he was walking them toward the government van. I advised him I was on my way to help him, since at the time of the frisk and loading up are the most dangerous for the agent.

As I was walking toward the van at a frisk pace I heard Rudy's voice on the radio "Vic, help me"! I took off at a dead run toward the van, when I came up on a mob of aliens with Rudy in the middle of them. He was almost defenseless since he was trying to keep them from taking his service pistol away from him. He was succeeding in defending his weapon but he was taking a pretty good beating from the aliens.

As I came upon them they never saw me as I started striking out at them with my wakie. Each one only took one blow as the talkie is a pretty good weapon. After a few minutes of close combat with the persistent aliens they were all subdued and on the ground. We loaded the bleeding bunch of attackers into the van and then Rudy found his voice. "They jumped me Vic, I guess they were going to kill me" he said. Yes, Rudy Lopez who normally would not hurt any one had had a close call. And my wakie talkie, well it never worked again!

CHAPTER 43

The Goodyear Eagle Tire Incident

The Border Patrol normally had a good fleet of cruisers and they are equipped well most of the time and with our own maintenance shop nearby the autos are pretty efficient. This happens most of the time as the mechanics maintain the fleet in good running order. That came handy one day and it proved to me that the maintenance of the cruisers was very important.

Agent Rolando Cruz and I were observing traffic on IH-35 near the famous Callahan Ranch when we spotted a car headed north that was extremely loaded and it gave us the probable cause to execute a stop for immigration purposes. I got behind the suspected auto and began the process of calling in the license plates when the driver made a quick beeline toward the right side and over the access road, through the fence line, and into the grassy pasture.

The Border Patrol service policy is that at no time would we pursue into the ranch land after an absconded vehicle. We are to stand fast at the penetrated hole in the fence and pursuit on foot if it is necessary. Since there was still some daylight left and we could see perfectly we stood by the hole in the ranch fence as the smuggler proceeded into the grassy pasture. There were no trees in the pasture and we could see clearly that the driver opened the car door to jump out. He did so as the car continued to move forward but then started to go to the right as if in a circle. It was not long before the car came back to the original spot where the driver had jumped out in the tall grass. There was a loud crunch sound heard and a human yell, and we knew that the car had found its missing driver. The car then came to a stop.

Cruz and I walked over to where the sound had come from and there was the driver complaining of a terrible stomach ache, and accusing me of running over him. We called an ambulance for the man and he went to get medical attention. The next morning I was the talk of the town as the driver was accusing me of running over him with the patrol car. The Mexican Consul Citlali Garcia was pictured with the alien smuggler on the front page of the Laredo Times who was displaying a tire print on his tummy. I was not moved by the accusations as I knew that I had followed service policy and not entered the ranch in question. An investigation was conducted and it was ascertained that the patrol car I was driving had brand new Goodyear Eagles tires on it and the mark on the alien's tummy was some other brand. I was cleared of the charges and he went on to jail.

CHAPTER 44

The Shooting Incident in South Laredo

One evening the entire shift met at Danny's Restaurant Downtown for a cup of coffee before setting out to our assigned areas for the evening. We were there having a good chat when a call came in that they had spotted a large U-Hual Truck in the area near El Cenizo. That was my assigned area for the evening so my partner B.J. Adams and I headed that way since it would take us about thirty minutes to get to that location. On the way we arrested seven aliens that were hiding on the side of the road. I called for someone to come and pick them up in case we got tied up looking for the big truck. Agent Raul Guerra responded he was in the general area and would take the aliens off our hands

Several days before a farmer named Bud Mckendrick had complained that he was approached by several men who wanted to use his farm on the river to do something or other. The farmer told them to leave the premises. He was woken up later that night as someone was shooting his dogs with a machine gun. All his protective dogs had been executed. I had a feeling that this is where they had spotted the big rental truck.

The Mckendrick Farm sat right on the Rio Grande and a crucial crossing point for aliens and drugs. There was a county maintained gravel road that led from the river to Highway 83 South. B.J. Adams was a tall trim agent that liked to run about five miles a day to keep in shape.

As we approached the gravel road that led from the highway to the river's edge we spotted a large U-Hual Truck approaching the highway. It appeared heavily loaded and was moving slow. I positioned the Border Patrol van I was driving as if to block the truck from getting on H-83S. The big truck kept on coming toward us and we could see two individuals riding in the front seat and no one else was visible. Maybe there were more in the cargo type box.

As the truck got closer I made a hand signal for them to pull over. Instead the driver accelerated the engine and went past our location and got on the highway. As I cranked up to give chase the driver rolled the big truck on to its side and into a large ditch that was there. B.J. and I could hear the women and children yelling that we assumed were in the cargo box of the truck. The two men riding in front scaled out the passenger window and jumped to the ground and started running back toward the river.

As B.J. Adams started to give chase and there was no doubt in my mind that he could overtake the men running I stopped him. I told him to take care of the injured people and call for help. I would give chase to the two smugglers fleeing into the brush line on the river side of the highway. I knew I could not overtake these men on foot so I took after them in the van. Since the road the truck had been was paralleling the route the two men were taking, I overtook them quickly. I could see that the two were hiding behind a small mesquite bush and as I approached the clearing I noticed what they were doing. They were breathing heavily and one was using the other to steady himself as he pointed a black semiautomatic at me.

I quickly pulled out my Smith and Wesson .357 that I was carrying and fired three quick rounds out of the passenger side window toward the gunman. I saw him fly like a wounded rabbit and hit the ground and remain there. The other smuggler disappeared into the brush and darkness was also setting in. I was furious because he had tried to shoot me, and then there was the aliens in the van he night have hit.

I walked over to him as he laid there on the ground and picked him up and took him toward the van parked on the gravel road. When I got to the fence that I did not remember crossing he started to resist and

I threw him through a hole in the fence and he landed at Agent Raul Guerra's feet. Raul Guerra had arrived just in time to help me with this wounded guy. As Raul picked him up and handcuffed him I could see a hole in his leg completely through. We got him into the van as Raul transferred the aliens to his van. I went back to check on my young partner and found him and some other agents from the shift giving first aid to the many aliens that were hurt when the man rolled the truck over. It had been a long afternoon.

I got to the office and was met with Chief Larry Teverbaugh at the back door. He said "Vic, call your wife and tell her that you are O.K. and do your paperwork, I'll take care of the news media", this man was a real leader. I did my paperwork and went home to my wife and kids.

The next morning I went in to go over the paperwork one more time and the FBI was waiting for me. Senior Agent Roger de la Garza and a rookie agent escorted me to the site of the shooting. First they asked me for my gun and went over it, writing the caliber and serial number. The gun was mine so they gave it back to me. They asked me where exactly I had shot the smuggler and I pointed to a small mesquite and they looked for the smugglers gun there. Not finding it, they asked me if I was sure on the location at which time I reached over and picked up a wad of flesh that was on the ground and gave it to them.

I was cleared of any wrong doing by the FBI.

CHAPTER 45

Run Ruffel Run

The area near the International Bridges in Laredo is usually full of illegal activity as the aliens that are not legally admitted by the Inspectors at the bridges attempt to cross into the U.S. anyway. The smugglers and thieves and sometimes rapists attempt to make a quick buck off these people. That was the case one after noon as Agent Harry Ruffel and I were working below the Ports of Entry.

That afternoon I was called in by the Chief to tell me that I had been cleared by the FBI of any wrong doing in the shooting of the smuggler in South Laredo. He did joke around that he was hoping he would not have to take my pistol away for being too quick on the trigger. I told him that the way I saw things I was not going to be run off the river. I was getting paid to guard the border and that is what I was doing.

He looked at Harry and joked "Keep an eye on him Harry". So Harry Ruffel and I left to go to the river and do our job. We parked a few blocks away and proceeded to go to the Sewer Plant and start checking the crossings up river near the new Port of Entry. It was not long before we heard talking coming from the river's edge. As we got to a clearing there in plain view was a man named Gonzalez who was a regular river bandit robbing two aliens. He was using two Doberman type dogs on a leach and holding the aliens at bay.

My reaction was to yell at him to stop it. He turned toward me and having some kind of quick release on the dogs let them go at me. I could hear the mangy curs barking and coming toward us so I turned to run and ran into Harry Ruffel who was walking right behind me. I knocked him down and I knew he did not stand a chance to run and get away from the dogs. I turned back toward the animals and drew my .357 pistol and as they lunged at us, I emptied my gun dropping both of them. The curs were dead but Harry was OK so that was good. I looked for the two aliens who had made good their escape and Gonzalez was already swimming the river and was about half-way to Mexico.

The shots had brought out the Mexico Immigration Officers to the River Banks and they arrested Gonzalez only to let him go later. As we drove into the Border Patrol Station I was summoned to the Chief's Office. There Chief Teverbaugh greeted me with a smile and pointed toward a very wet looking Gonzalez who yelled, "That's him Chief, that's the Officer that tried to kill me". The Chief had a few words with Gonzalez and asked him to leave the Station.

Chief Teverbaugh then addressed me "What am I going to do with you and that trigger finger of yours", he said. You have been involved in two shootings in one week". I knew that the Chief was at odds what to do with me for doing my job. He finally said he was going to promote me to Intelligence Officer and I would be part of his staff. And so I left the field and the work I loved so much.

CHAPTER 46

Rudy and the Hobo

After spending three years in the Intelligence Office I promote to Anti-Smuggling Investigations (Special Agent) at Laredo Sector. The Anti-Smuggling Unit consisted of 9-10 Special Agents and a Supervisor. The functions of the agents were to investigate the cases arrested by the Border Patrol Agents and take them as far as possible to insure maximum prosecutions of the smugglers. Sometimes it involved investigating the links between a certain smuggler and other well known smuggling organizations. It also involved doing surveillance on the subjects to make further arrests on a certain smuggling ring.

On this day Special Agent Rudy Lopez and I were doing surveillance on a plaza in Laredo and a nearby convinance store where smugglers frequented. Rudy and I had worked together since our uniform days and we got along very well to the point that we socialized with our wives and kids at times. I had seen his girls Courtney and Christine grow up and his wife Carol and Linda got along fine.

On this day I parked at the McDonalds parking lot next to a large dumpster where the employees dumped refuse from the restaurant. About noon we saw a vagrant approach the dumpster and start pulling bags out to search for food. From one bag he would pull out half-eaten burger and from other he would pull out half cups of sodas. He started to place those items of interest on the side walk as if forming a platoon of soldiers. It was obvious this man was getting ready to have a buffet of the left over food.

After making his selections the man sat down on the curb in front of our car and started to dine. He was quite noisy about the whole thing because he knew we were watching him and could hear all that he said. He would pick up a bitten fish sandwich and out loud proclaim how much he liked fish sandwiches, polish it off and then he would wash it down with a drink. This ceremony went on for several minutes as he would pick up a half of a burger and fries and relish it before he ate it and of course he would wash it down with another half drink from the row he had there in the curb.

Finally, Rudy had had enough and jumped out the car and approached the vagrant. He reached into his pocket and pulled out a five dollar bill and stretched his hand to give it to the man. He said " Here man, go get yourself a real meal". The Hobo's eyes lit up as if he had discovered gold. "Have a real meal, hell man, I already ate, it is time for a bottle of Thunderbird wine." At that the man grabbed the five dollar bill and ran to the corner store to spend his fortune.

I had seen enough, I drove off and stopped at a nearby restaurant to have lunch. I ordered but Rudy just looked at the menu. I asked him what was wrong and he quickly answered that the five dollars he gave the Hobo was all Carol had given him in the morning when he went to work. Well, lunch was on me that day!

CHAPTER 47

The Dr. Ciro Lopez Story

In 1986 Congress passed the Immigration Reform Act (IRCA) with aims at controlling the flow of illegal aliens by giving those already here the opportunity to legalize after qualifying on some very weak issues. First the aliens must prove that they had worked especially in farm labor for a specified term. They must present some proof that they had done so and pass a medical exam and pay a small fee. Little did the Congress realize that they were going to open the doors for millions of illegal aliens to get legalize, the majority who did not qualify at all.

Soon Legalization Offices were opened in most border cities and some larger cities in the country. Laredo was one city chosen to have an office. At first the office was opened at the Port of Entry and later it was moved to a location on Saunders where there was more parking and it was more accessible to the applicants. From day one the program was wide open for corruption.

The Chief Legalization Officer appointed to run the program was a former U.S. Consular Officer, Victor Abeyta who would oversee the entire operation from Mexico City. The qualifying aliens would be inspected by a medical doctor to insure that they did not carry a disease that would jeopardize the people in the U.S. Doctors along the Mexican Border were handpicked by Abeyta to screen the aliens to insure only healthy ones were admitted. All was running well until one day, I received a call from our Orlando, Florida Office that they had a situation on their hands and needed me to investigate further to see what was going on.

The agents in Florida claimed that a group of aliens were taken to a local farm and dropped off to work for a certain farmer. When the farmer's wife woke up and found a van load of workers ready to go to work but her husband had been dead for five years and the farm had been sold she wanted them removed from her property. Well the aliens did not want to leave since they had gone to a great expense to get there.

I asked the agents in Florida to send me at least one alien so that I could interview him without going to Florida myself. After several weeks Panfilo Hernandez arrived via U.S. Marshal's custody. I went to the Webb county jail to interview him and this was his story. A man had gone to his hometown in the mountains in Southern Mexico, looking for men who wanted to come to work in the U.S. legally for a fee. He liked the idea but the recruiter told him to gather a group of fifty and he would send a bus to bring them to N. Laredo where they would be issued a "permit" to work in this country. He got a group of fifty together and called the recruiter who as promised sent a bus to bring them to N. Laredo, Tamaulipas, Mexico. They were taken to the clinic of Dr. Ciro Lopez and dropped off.

At the clinic the aliens were given a packet that needed only their name and biographical data to be complete. They were rehearsed by the Doctor's secretaries as to the information that had already been filled out on the packet until they had memorized it. They paid their fee to the Doctor to include the physical that was never performed. Then they were marched to the Port of Entry where there was a long line of applicants, but their names were called out by the security guard and taken to the front of the line.

They were processed into the U.S. and taken by the same guide to a van that was waiting for them and away they went to Florida. None of them had ever been in this country nor worked in the agricultural areas in Florida like their packet said. All that information had been filled by the doctor's secretaries. They had seen the doctor only sitting on top of a desk at his clinic telling the secretaries what to do.

I knew that what we had here was a massive case of fraud and corruption. My question was if the employees of the Legalization Office were involved. I grabbed my trusty partner, Rudy Lopez and we went to pay the Office a visit. As soon as I walked in the door of the Legalization Office at the Port of Entry, the employee that had being designated as in charge stood up and approached me. "What the hell are you doing here" yelled Juan Meza the employee. "I came for a small visit", I replied. "Well get the hell out of here, this is my office and it runs the way I want it to run", he continued. At that time the security guard was coming in from the outside circumventing the line with a group of aliens.

I was shocked at the behavior displayed by Mr. Meza and something told me that there was something wrong at that office and this man was right in the middle of it. At that time I was doing a separate IRCA investigation into the activities of a man named Juan Moncada from Greely Colorado. This man was falsifying the status of aliens to qualify them for benefits under the new law. We knew he was operating from a modest motel called the Evylyn here in Laredo.

One night Special Agent Joe Martinez and I were doing surveillance on his room at the motel. We could see people coming and going from the room when we observed Mr. Juan Meza from the Legalization Office emerge from the room and he was conversing with Juan Moncada. Why would the man from the Legalization Office be meeting with a known legalization violator. I requested the telephone tolls of the Meza residence and was shocked to find out that at 15 minutes after five Meza would place a call to the office of Dr. Ciro Lopez every day.

I requested help from the Office of Professional Responsibility and Integrity and they said they would be coming in a few days. Meanwhile Joe and I arrested Moncada when he was transporting some unqualified aliens to the Legalization Office. None of the aliens qualified for benefits and they also had a packet from the Mexican Doctor.

Moncada was a tough cookie to get to cooperate but in running a records check in Mexico we found out he was wanted for murdering a public servant in Southern Mexico. Now he decided to cooperate since he did not want to face murder charges in Mexico. He quickly admitted that he and the Doctor and Meza had a little business going. Moncada would recruit aliens in the interior of Mexico and bring them to the border where the Doctor would fabricate the health forms and provide a packet and then Meza would allow them into the country. They had a nice business going.

Moncada decided that he needed to cooperate with us to get a lighter sentence. Office of Professional Responsibility and Integrity had two Immigration Officers from El Paso come to Laredo to pretend to be undocumented aliens and be introduced by Moncada to Meza. The next day the two Immigration Officers went though the system and became "Legalized". That afternoon Meza came to the motel room and in the presence of the two Officers accepted four hundred dollars from Moncada for the transaction. He also said he guaranteed his services and departed the room because he was on his way to class at the college. When he got into his high rise truck Joe Martinez and I were there guns drawn and made the arrest.

We went to federal court and Mr. Meza had some of Laredo's best criminal lawyers defending him. I think the clincher in his case was not only the testimony from Moncada but also the telephone tolls from Meza's house to the Doctors clinic every after noon at the same time. On this phone call the Doctor would give Meza the list of aliens that would be ready for the next day and therefore the aliens could be called to the front of the waiting line. Judge James Kazen asked Meza if he had ever talked to the Doctor and he answered—No. Testimony from some of the Legalization Office indicated the Doctor would pay daily visits to the Office and had the roam of the house, he also would bring his secretaries to bring food for the employees of the Office. The Federal Judge was not fooled by the answers that Meza gave.

Now that the inside man, Juan Meza and the recruiter Juan Moncada were under arrest I had the two big fish to go after, Dr. Ciro Lopez and Victor Abeyta. Dr. Lopez was not about to come to the U.S. side unless it was something important. Victor Abeyta was in Mexico City insulated by his many friends who did not believe he was a corrupt government official. Meanwhile the infiltration of not qualifying aliens had slowed down to a trickle. I still managed to take down 129 small fish that were trying their best to get aliens into the country before the window closed on IRCA.

One day I received a call to the office from Dr. Ciro Lopez who asked me to drop the investigation on him because he thought I was a nice person and he wanted to be my friend. I kept thinking that Juan Meza had been a nice person too until the Doctor had steered him wrong, enough for Meza to forget his oath.

I requested help from Washington to go after Victor Abeyta and they sent an internal affairs investigator who was an expert in government corruption cases. We traveled to Farmington New Mexico to do a financial investigation on Abeyta since that was his home of record. Abeyta had a small sheep farm outside Farmington but there was no indication that huge amounts of money were being invested on it. We went to Farmington and served a subpoena on his bank. The Bank President seemed cooperative but he was really not. He did assign one of the officers a Mary Bales to get us what ever we needed to finish the investigation.

The banker did tell me that Abeyta was his personal friend and he did not agree with the investigation. He proved his friendship to Abeyta when he heard me ask Mary Bales where the bathrooms were and he answered that they were four blocks away at the McDonalds. He did say to be careful because the frozen ground could be dangerous. I quit drinking coffee for the duration of the investigation. We did uncover where Abeyta had cashed some checks from Dr. Ciro Lopez.

I knew that it was going to be hard to apprehend the Mexican Doctor. He was not just going to come over and turn himself in. By now I had estimated that he had committed 12,500 cases of Immigration Fraud, no telling how many of those were carrying any disease that would be harmful to the residents of the U.S. since the aliens were not medically inspected. I walked over to the Mexican side of the Rio Grande and went to the Doctor's house at Colonia Longoria. I approached the house and the yard man quickly challenged my presence at the front yard fence. I told him I was looking for Dr. Lopez and the man quickly responded that if it was to get the papers to come to the U.S. to go see him at the office. While I was talking to him I softly repeated the license plates of all the family cars into my tape recorder.

On the way back to the U.S., I stopped at the Port Of Entry and entered the plates into the computer lookouts. The next day the lookouts started to come in. Most of the hits were on a Suburban driven by a young woman presumably the Doctors wife. All the entries were made at about one in the afternoon. Agent Rudy Lopez and I decided to go sit by the Port and follow the vehicle when the Officers alerted us that it was coming in. We were not disappointed as the Suburban entered driven by the young woman and drove straight to Kiddieland Academy a preschool private school.

I called Kiddie Land Academy and asked them when their graduation was going to be. The director Mrs. Garcia advised me that the graduation would be the next day at La Posada Hotel. She said that the event was sold out as all the parents would be there to see their children graduate. She said all seats at the dinner were reserved by name on the table. I could not have asked for more. I went to the banquet hall at La Posada and found where the good doctor would be sitting.

The next night I gathered some of the Special Agents and a Police Lieutenant named Ismael Alardin. I advised the Policeman that he was to go into the banquet and approach the Doctor and inform him his Suburban was broken into and that he had the man in custody but he needed to file a complaint against the man. It worked well and the Doctor told Lt. Alardin that if there was something he could not stand was thieves. As Lt. Alardin and the Doctor stepped out of the banquet hall and near the street, I stepped out the darkness. "Good evening Doctor Lopez, I'm Victor Villarreal and I'm here to welcome you to the United States". At that time Agent Frank Torres handcuffed a very pale man and placed him in one of our cars.

Neither Juan Meza nor Dr. Ciro Lopez testified against Victor Abeyta and there was not enough evidence to prosecute the former Consular Officer. In the end Meza and Lopez went to prison and Abeyta went free.

CHAPTER 48

The Pedro Dominguez
Corruption Case

Of the nine or so Special Agents assigned to the Anti Smuggling Office in Laredo, one was an older Agent who had been around over twenty years in the Border Patrol and was part of the Investigations Office. Although he had been in the Office for years I could not recall a single case he had completed. He just hung around the office or would disappear sometimes months at a time. Management did not seemed to care enough to look for him or make the man accountable for his time like they did the rest of us. The usual answer was that he was working with DEA on a very important case. One day the DEA people called looking for him as they had not seen him for months either. He would be seen only at the gas pump as he filled his car with gas.

I always suspected he was up to no good but if management did not care, who was I to question their judgment. One day an Immigration Supervisor named Rogelio Salinas called me and said someone was issuing entry permits with his stamp and using his initials. The Supervisor said that Inspectors were intercepting aliens with the bogus permits and it was causing some of them to suspect that he was issuing them out for money. He pled with me to open an investigation into the matter to clear the problem up.

I did open an investigation targeting whoever was printing these permits up to ease the pressure it was creating on Rogelio Salinas. He did inform me that one day the Immigration Stamp that was assigned to him had been stolen from the Immigration Counter at the Port of Entry. A new one had been issued to him but the old one was never recovered. At that time two aliens were detained at the bridge using the bogus permits.

I went down to the Port of Entry and interrogated the two men. Although they were cooperative they could only tell me they had paid two hundred dollars for each permit and had bought them from a man in N. Laredo named Julian. They said that that man named Julian had called his connection at the Immigration Office and given him the information over the phone and within an hour the man had arrived with the documents. They described him as an older man in a brown car with black top. They could provide no more than that information.

A couple of days later Border Patrol Agents at the IH-35 Checkpoint intercepted a family of four that were displaying the same documents as the two previous arrests. The permits also had the Rogelio Salinas stamp on them and the initials R.S. They were from the same batch of numbers as the previous. I set up a lookout to try to intercept more permits in hopes of getting to the bottom of the case. When the four aliens were brought to the Investigations Office they told the same story with one new twist. They were given the permits on this side of the Rio Grande since they had already crossed when they were recruited to buy the bogus permits.

They claimed they were taken to an apartment on Santa Maria Street and to the apartment where the provider lived with his wife and small boy. The family consisted of a man, his wife and two children. The man said that the insider that was providing the permits to the vendor was an older man in a brown car with black top. When the family was brought to the Investigations Office at the Laredo Border Patrol Sector which was located at the back part of the government facility the man said, "There is the car parked right there!" and he was pointing at my government car. Everyone got a laugh out of that comment since he had mentioned it was an older man also.

Boy, I thought, that in trying to get some pressure away from Rogelio Salinas, I now had some evidence pointing to me. The man also remembered that the provider of the documents and the man he had paid the money was named Julian Banda. To add to a worsening situation that was the name that fit one of my Confidential Informants. I had Joe Martinez call my informant Julian Band and ask him to come to the office. I had Joe call him because I was furious at the man. When he came in we took him straight to the interrogation room and closed the door. I told him straight out that he was going to jail for selling permits to undeserving aliens for money.

He quickly admitted his part in the illegal scheme. He said he was hurting for money and on one visit to our office he had been recruited by the "Old man" to deliver some documents for him and before long he joined the crooked operation. When he said "Old man" Joe and Vito Ramirez who had stepped into the room looked at me because everyone knew who the old man was. It was one of our Special Agents named Pedro Dominguez. It all made sense know because he and I drove identical Chevrolet Impalas that were brown with black tops. Meanwhile Dominguez had retired from government service a few days before.

I quickly telephoned the Office of Professional Integrity in McAllen, Texas and they dispatched two Special Agents to Laredo for the Arrest of Pedro Dominguez. Meanwhile Joe Martinez, Rudy Lopez, Vito Ramirez and I went to work to set up a trap to catch a corrupt former government officer. We were able to get Julian Banda to cooperate and telephone Dominguez that he had two more clients for permits. Dominguez agreed to come by the Informants' apartment and drop them later in the evening. We went to the apartment and set up recording devices to catch the conversations between Dominguez and Banda.

Once everything was ready as we waited for nightfall and the two OIG Agents to come in from McAllen to make the arrest of Dominguez. The two agents arrived in the nick of time, actually Dominguez was already on the way out from his house, when they arrived. I briefed them quickly and we took our positions. We had to be careful as Dominguez carried a .45 caliber automatic.

Well, Dominguez arrived to make the drop of documents to the Informant. They conversed a few minutes and then Dominguez picked up his money and started to leave when we arrested him. It was ironic because he had been retired for only five days. We took him back to the Informants' apartment and read him his rights and handcuffed him. Pedro kept looking at me and finally he spoke and said, " Vic, you think that you are so smart and there you are all nervous and look at me, I'm as cool as a cucumber".

"Pete, you might be as cool as a cucumber but tonight you are going to sleep in jail, and I maybe nervous as you say, but I think I'm more embarrassed than anything because you were one of us and now you are one of them". With that said, we took him to jail and booked him.

We went back to the office to write the affidavit for a warrant to search the Dominguez' home. We wrote the affidavit and went to secure Pete's house as we got the warrant signed. It was about midnight when one of the Dominguez's neighbors showed up, a Mr. Galo Garcia who was coming in from a party. He recognized me and went over and said, "Don't tell me you arrested Pedro". At that, most of the agents surrounding the house laughed . It would be another three hours before we located the U.S. Magistrate, Marcel Notzon to sign the Search Warrant.

As we entered the home we went straight to the master bedroom and right there in plain sight was a government IBM that had been missing from our office for several years. In the closet of the bedroom was a file cabinet with the missing Immigration Stamp, blank immigration permits ready to be filled out, and a bag full of Border Patrol Agents badges to include three badges for Chief Patrol Agent.

Also there were several sensor maps originals, and the stencils for an underground Newspaper called "Farter's Hinds" that had haunted the Sector Staff for years. There were boxes of professionally made bumper stickers insulting the Sector Chief. These stickers had been found on traffic signs and buildings throughout the city. The most damaging of all was a tablet where Dominguez had a list of wholesalers throughout the country that were selling "His" permits. The list included how much each one owed to Dominguez and other damaging comments.

And so former Special Agent Pedro Dominguez was found guilty and sentenced but the Informant was not sentenced because of his cooperation on the case. Sometime after that whether connected to the case or not Julian Banda was found in the Rio Grande with two cement blocks tied to his feet, and the fish had had a feast on the man.

CHAPTER 49

Conclusion

While working for the Border Patrol I continued my Military service in reserve status and after what seemed like many summer camps in the U.S. and one in Germany and after being promoted to Lt. Colonel with twenty six good years out of thirty, I retired. I had attended the Quartermaster Career Course in Ft. Lee, Virginia, and also taught ten different cycles of officers there. I also attended the Command and Staff College and had taught eight cycles of officers at Ft. Bliss and Ft. Sill Oklahoma. I had continued to attend college and after receiving my Bachelors Degree. I also received my Masters Degree at Laredo State University.

Capt. Brittingham and Lt. Kopec at a recent reunion

General Stoner greets Capt. Victor M. Villarreal after
arriving in Frankfort Germany with the 850th Collection
and Classification Company from Laredo, Texas.

In the Border Patrol I had been promoted to Senior Special Agent
and had enjoyed that grade the last ten years of my career. I attempted
to promote higher but I had not moved to other cities or I had failed to
kiss the right baby. I had been assigned to DEA to work with them for
several years, first by being present at their office and then by being on
call. I also met several outstanding agents there.

My wife was doing well as a teacher and school administrator so I
am proud of her. My two sons had done very well in high school football
being selected for All District Honors their Senior Year, and now they
were both college graduates and with good jobs. Victor Jr. is employed
by the U.S. Border Patrol and Marco Antonio is as Civil Engineer in
Chicago.

After retiring from the Border Patrol I have taught at Laredo
Community College Government classes and at LBJ High School I
taught Criminal Justice. I had obtained a Real Estate Brokers License

and own a small ranch. I was real proud to have served in the U.S. Army and with one of the most famous divisions the 1st Air Cavalry and also served with the U.S. Border Patrol. All things considered it has been a good life and I love this country. I hope I have made the right actions to show how much I love this country.

Thanks Dad for bringing us to the United States.

Our son Marco Antonio Villarreal graduation from
Texas A&M School of Engineering, 2003.

Victor Jr. and Victor Sr. at his graduation from the Border
Patrol Academy, Artesia, New Mexico Feb.2009.

Charlie Bader and Victor Villarreal at the 1st Cavalry
Luncheon at Killeen, Texas.2009 Reunion.

Victor and Linda's engagement, after the Viet-Nam War. 1969.

Lt. Victor M. Villarreal at a Martin High School
ROTC Awards Presentation 1970.

The End.

About the Author

Victor M. Villarreal was born in Northern Mexico at Rancho El Ebano, Sabinas Hidalgo, Nuevo Leon, Mexico in 1947. He attended school in Mexico for a couple of years and then the family immigrated to the United States going to live in a small Texas town by the name of Big Wells, Texas. After living there for a few years the family joined the migrant stream following the farm crops from Texas to Fort Wayne Indiana. After living on a farm outside Fort Wayne the family relocated to Fremont, California where they lived for several years, each winter returning to Mexico for a spell. After several years of going back and forth to California his father returned to Mexico and his mother and he and sister Lilia moved to Laredo where he attended Jr. High and High School.

Upon Graduation from High School, Victor was inducted into the Armed Services, where he had the opportunity to attend Infantry Officers School and graduated as a Commissioned Officer in the Army. He was assigned to duty at Ft. Bliss Texas where he served training basic trainees during the Viet-Nam War. He attended Jungle Experts School in Panama before departing for Viet-Nam. In Viet-Nam he was assigned to the 1st Cavalry Division where he served as an Infantry Platoon Leader and Company Commander. For the last few months in combat he served as S-3 Air for the 2nd Battalion of the 12th Cavalry.

Victor was decorated for his service in combat with the Siler Star, Bronze Star with V and Bronze Star, two Air Medals, one Purple Heart, the Army Commendation Medal, the Combat Infantry Badge and several other medals for service in a combat zone. After the war and after holding several jobs he was hired by the U.S. Border Patrol, stationed in Laredo, Texas his entire career. He attended college at Laredo State University earning a Bachelors in Political Science and a Masters in Interdisciplinary Science.

He retired from the Border Patrol as the Border Organized Coordinator and from the Army Reserve as a Lt. Colonel.